The Ultimate Guide to Building a Successful Massage Therapy Business

Maurice Hill

Disclaimer:

This book is intended for informational purposes only, and should not be construed as legal, financial, or professional advice. The author and publisher make no representations or warranties with respect to the accuracy, completeness, or suitability of the information contained herein, and will not be liable for any damages, losses, or claims arising from the use of or reliance on the information provided in this book.

Readers are advised to consult with qualified professionals, such as attorneys, accountants, or financial advisors, for specific advice and guidance on legal, financial, or professional matters related to their freight brokerage business.

The information provided in this book is based on the authors' research, expertise, and experience, and may not reflect the latest industry trends, regulations, or practices. The authors and publisher do not endorse or promote any specific products, services, or companies mentioned in this book, and readers are advised to conduct their own due diligence before making any business decisions or investments.

By reading this book, readers agree to release and hold harmless the authors and publisher from any liability or claims arising from the use of or reliance on the information provided herein.

We hope that our collective expertise and insights have provided valuable guidance and support for readers of this book, and we welcome your feedback and suggestions for future editions.

Dedication

To each and every massage therapist who entered the field with a sincere desire to help people improve their health and well-being,

This book is dedicated to you. Your unwavering commitment to the art of healing touch, your compassionate hearts, and your dedication to the well-being of others have inspired the creation of this guide. It is through your hands that individuals find comfort, relief, and a path to holistic wellness.

You have chosen a profession that goes beyond the physical, reaching into the realms of emotional and spiritual healing. Your presence, empathy, and skill have the power to transform lives. From easing the burdens of stress and pain to promoting relaxation and rejuvenation, you bring comfort to those who seek solace in your therapeutic touch.

Your work extends far beyond the massage table. You are listeners, healers, and pillars of support. You create spaces of trust, empathy, and compassion where individuals can find respite from the challenges of everyday life. With each session, you leave an indelible mark on the lives of your clients, bringing a sense of balance, serenity, and renewed vitality.

Through your dedication, you have embarked on a journey that is both challenging and rewarding. The path of a massage therapist demands continuous learning, growth, and self-care. It requires resilience, compassion, and an unwavering commitment to excellence. It is through your genuine desire to help others that you have become catalysts for positive change in the lives of countless individuals.

May this guide serve as a source of inspiration, guidance, and empowerment as you navigate the intricacies of building a successful massage therapy business. It is my sincere hope that the knowledge, strategies, and insights shared within these pages will equip you with the tools necessary to thrive in an ever-evolving industry. May it strengthen your skills, ignite your passion, and deepen your impact on the well-being of those you serve.

To each and every massage therapist, your dedication and profound impact on the lives of others deserve recognition and gratitude. Thank you for choosing a path of healing, for being the guiding light in the journeys of wellness and self-discovery, and for embodying the true essence of compassionate care.

Acknowledgment

I would like to express my heartfelt gratitude to the incredible massage therapists around the world who tirelessly dedicate themselves to the art of healing touch. Your passion, expertise, and commitment to bringing relief and promoting well-being through therapeutic massage have inspired the creation of this guide. It is through your hands and compassionate hearts that individuals find solace, rejuvenation, and profound healing. Your tireless efforts are truly commendable.

I would also like to extend my appreciation to the remarkable research team at One United Publishing. Your dedication, expertise, and meticulous efforts have been instrumental in bringing this guide to life. Your commitment to thorough research, attention to detail, and passion for delivering accurate and valuable information have ensured the quality and integrity of this publication. Your contributions are invaluable and have made a significant impact on the depth and credibility of the content within these pages.

To all the massage therapists who generously shared their experiences and insights during the research process, thank you for your openness and willingness to contribute to the collective knowledge of the massage therapy community. Your wisdom, anecdotes, and expertise have enriched this guide and made it a comprehensive resource that reflects the diverse perspectives and experiences within the industry.

I would also like to express my gratitude to the educators, mentors, and industry professionals who have dedicated their time and expertise to shaping the massage therapy field. Your guidance and support have been instrumental in the development of this guide, providing valuable insights and best practices that have shaped its content.

To my family and friends, thank you for your unwavering support and encouragement throughout this journey. Your belief in me and the importance of this project has been a constant source of motivation and inspiration.

Lastly, to the readers of this guide, thank you for embarking on this journey with me. It is my sincere hope that the knowledge and strategies shared within these pages will empower you to build a successful massage therapy business, create meaningful connections with your clients, and make a positive impact on the well-being of others.

Contents

Preface

As I embark on the journey of writing The Ultimate Guide to Building a Successful Massage Therapy Business, I draw inspiration from personal experiences and a deep-rooted passion for supporting massage therapists in their quest for professional success. Over the years, I have encountered talented massage therapists who possess extraordinary skills in their craft. However, due to a lack of business knowledge, they have faced the unfortunate reality of seeking alternative means of income. This realization, combined with my background as a founder and CEO of multiple businesses, compelled me to create this guide—an avenue through which I can share my business training and experiences to empower entrepreneurs in the massage therapy field.

Massage therapy holds immense potential to enhance people's lives, offering an array of benefits that include stress reduction, anxiety relief, pain management, improved sleep, and overall well-being. Through my encounters with fellow wounded military veterans, I have witnessed how massage therapy has become an integral part of their well-being journey. From aiding in the recovery of physical injuries to facilitating emotional healing and stress relief, massage therapy has played a vital role in their overall wellness. These personal encounters have instilled in me a profound appreciation for the transformative power of touch and therapeutic techniques on an individual level.

However, from the standpoint of the massage therapy entrepreneur, the path to building a successful business is not without its challenges. Massage therapists often face obstacles unique to their profession. The physical demands of the job can take a toll on their own well-being and longevity in the field. Moreover, navigating the realms of competition, marketing, and advertising poses its own set of hurdles. It is my firm belief that by equipping massage therapists with the necessary business knowledge, we can empower them to overcome these challenges and flourish in their practice.

"The Ultimate Guide to Building a Successful Massage Therapy Business" aims to address the business concerns head-on. Each chapter of this guide delves into key aspects of entrepreneurship, offering practical strategies, expert advice, and real-life examples. From defining business goals and creating a comprehensive business plan to establishing a strong brand, effectively marketing services, and providing exceptional client experiences, this guide serves as a comprehensive roadmap to success.

By leveraging my business training, experiences, and passion for the field, I aspire to bridge the gap between exceptional massage therapy skills and the business acumen necessary to thrive in a competitive industry. I want to empower massage therapists to not only provide exceptional services but also build sustainable and profitable businesses that enable them to create a lasting impact on the lives of their clients.

I invite you, fellow entrepreneurs in the massage therapy field, to join me on this transformative journey. Let us rise above the challenges, embrace our collective potential, and reshape the landscape of the massage therapy industry. Together, we can elevate the profession and ensure that talented and passionate individuals thrive while positively impacting the well-being of others.

Introduction

Massage therapy is an ancient healing art that has been practiced for thousands of years. Its benefits are widely recognized, including stress reduction, pain relief, and improved overall health and well-being. In recent years, the demand for massage therapy services has skyrocketed as more people seek natural and holistic treatments for their physical and emotional ailments. As a result, the massage therapy industry has become increasingly competitive, and it can be challenging for new businesses to stand out.

In this book, we will explore the strategies and tactics you need to build a successful massage therapy business. Whether you are a seasoned massage therapist looking to expand your practice or a new entrepreneur just starting out, this book will provide you with the tools and insights you need to succeed.

We will start by defining your business goals and creating a comprehensive business plan that outlines your strategies for success. From there, we will explore the key elements of branding, marketing, and promotion that will help you stand out in a crowded market.

We will also delve into the operational aspects of running a massage therapy business, including pricing and packaging your services, managing your finances, hiring and managing employees, and managing client relationships. You will learn the best practices

1

for providing high-quality services, building strong client relationships, and creating a sustainable work-life balance.

Throughout this book, we will provide you with practical advice, case studies, and real-world examples that will help you apply these strategies to your own massage therapy business. Our goal is to provide you with a comprehensive guide that will help you build a successful and sustainable massage therapy business that provides exceptional services and achieves long-term success and profitability.

Whether you are a new entrepreneur just starting out or an experienced massage therapist looking to take your business to the next level, this book will provide you with the insights and tools you need to succeed. We hope that you find this book informative, inspiring, and practical, and we look forward to helping you build the massage therapy business of your dreams.

Chapter One
Defining Your Business Goals

As a massage therapist, you may have decided to start your own business with the hopes of sharing your passion for healing and wellness with others. But before you can begin, defining your business goals is crucial. Why is this step so important? Well, simply put, having a clear understanding of your purpose and objectives will help guide all of your future decisions and actions. It will keep you focused, motivated, and on track toward success. So, take some time to reflect on why you started your business and what you hope to accomplish. Perhaps you want to help people relieve stress and anxiety, or you're passionate about sports massage and helping athletes recover from injuries. Whatever your reason, make sure it's clear in your mind.

Once you've defined your purpose, it's time to set clear goals and objectives. This means making them specific, measurable, achievable, relevant, and time-bound. Setting SMART goals will help you stay focused and ensure that you're making progress toward achieving your overall purpose. For example, you might set a goal to increase your revenue by 20% in the next year. This is a specific goal that is measurable, achievable, and time-bound. It's also relevant to your business because it will help you grow and sustain your business in the long term. Or perhaps you want to expand your client base by targeting a specific demographic. This is another SMART goal that is specific, measurable, achievable, relevant, and time-bound. It will help you focus your marketing efforts and ensure that you're reaching the right audience.

Finally, you need to identify your target audience. Who are the people you hope to serve through your massage therapy services? Understanding your target audience is crucial because it will help you create marketing strategies that resonate with them and tailor your services to meet their needs. For example, if you specialize in prenatal massage, your target audience may be pregnant women or new mothers. Or, if you focus on sports massage, your target audience may be athletes or fitness enthusiasts. Understanding your target audience can create a more effective marketing strategy and build a loyal client base. Here are some websites and software programs that can help with defining your business goals as a massage therapist:

- **Trello:** This project management tool can help you organize your goals and objectives in a visual way, making it easier to stay on track and achieve your targets.
- **Google Analytics:** This web analytics service can help you understand your target audience better by providing insights into their demographics, interests, and online behavior.
- **SurveyMonkey:** This online survey tool can help you gather

feedback from your clients and potential customers, allowing you to better understand their needs and preferences.

- **Canva:** This graphic design platform can help you create eye-catching marketing materials that resonate with your target audiences, such as social media graphics, flyers, and brochures.

- **HubSpot:** This all-in-one marketing software can help you create, manage, and track your marketing campaigns, allowing you to reach your target audience more effectively and efficiently.

Using these tools and platforms allows you to streamline your business goal-setting process and better understand your target audience, helping you build a successful and sustainable massage therapy business. In conclusion, defining your business goals is the first step to building a successful massage therapy business. Take the time to reflect on your purpose, set SMART goals, and identify your target audience. With a clear understanding of your objectives, you'll be well on your way to achieving your dreams and sharing your passion for healing with others.

Chapter Two
Creating a Business Plan

As a massage therapist, you have the power to heal and bring balance to your clients' lives. Starting your own business can be daunting, but with the right tools and resources, you can turn your passion into a successful and thriving business. This chapter will explore the importance of creating a business plan for your massage therapy business. A well-written business plan is essential for any business, and a massage therapy business is no exception. Your business plan provides a roadmap for your business and outlines your strategies for success. It helps you define your goals and objectives and provides a framework for making informed decisions that will impact your business's success.

In this chapter, we'll discuss the key elements of a business plan for your massage therapy business. From the executive summary to financial projections, we'll cover everything you need to know to create a comprehensive and effective business plan. We'll start by discussing the executive summary, which briefly overviews your business and its purpose. Then we'll dive into the company description, which provides a more detailed description of your business, including its mission, values, and goals. The market analysis section will help you assess your industry, including your competitors and target audience.

Next, we'll explore the service and product line section, which describes your massage therapy services, pricing, and packaging. We'll also discuss marketing and sales strategies, which will help you promote your business and attract new clients. Finally, we'll cover financial projections, including revenue, expenses, and profits. By the end of this chapter, you'll have a clear understanding of the importance of creating a business plan for your massage therapy business. You'll also have the tools and resources you need to create a comprehensive and effective plan to guide your business toward success. So, let's get started!

A business plan is a critical component of any successful massage therapy business. It provides a roadmap for your business, outlining your strategies for success and helping you make informed decisions that will impact your bottom line. But what exactly is a business plan, and why is it so essential? A business plan is a written document that outlines your business's goals, strategies, and financial projections. It includes everything from a company description to a market analysis and a detailed plan for marketing and sales. A well-written business plan is a comprehensive document that provides a clear picture of your business's operations and financial performance.

There are several benefits to creating a business plan for your massage therapy business. First and foremost, it provides a roadmap for your business, outlining your goals and strategies for achieving them. It helps you stay focused and on track toward success and provides a framework for making informed decisions that will impact your business's performance. A business plan also helps you attract investors or secure financing for your business. A well-written business plan can demonstrate to investors that you have a clear understanding of your industry and your target audience and that you have a solid plan for achieving your business goals. Additionally, a business plan can help you identify potential challenges and risks that may impact your business's success. By addressing these challenges and developing strategies to overcome them, you can mitigate risks and increase your chances of success.

To create a comprehensive business plan for your massage therapy business, you'll need to include several key elements. A typical business plan includes the following sections:

- **Executive Summary:** A brief overview of the entire plan that highlights the key points.
- **Company Description:** A more detailed description of the company, including its history, mission statement, and current operations.
- **Market Analysis:** An assessment of the industry, including market size, growth potential, and competition.

- **Service or Product Line:** A detailed description of the products or services offered, including pricing and packaging.

- **Marketing and Sales:** A plan for promoting the business and attracting customers, including market research, advertising, and sales strategies.

- **Financial Projections:** A projection of the company's financial performance over the next three to five years, including revenue, expenses, and profit.

- **Management and Organization:** A description of the company's organizational structure, including the management team and any key personnel.

- **Operations:** A plan for day-to-day operations, including production processes, supply chain management, and quality control.

- **SWOT Analysis:** An analysis of the company's strengths, weaknesses, opportunities, and threats.

- **Appendices:** Additional information, such as resumes of key personnel, licenses and permits, and other relevant documents.

Each section will be explained in more detail below:

Executive Summary

An executive summary is a brief overview of your massage

comprehensive overview of your business, including its history, mission, and vision. It should also outline your company's values, goals, and objectives. This section should provide an in-depth understanding of what your business does, why it exists, and how it plans to achieve its goals.

A well-written company description is essential for any massage therapy business because it provides a clear picture of what your business does and why it exists. It helps you define your business's purpose and objectives and provides a framework for making informed decisions that will impact your business's success. A company description also helps you stand out in a crowded market by highlighting your unique value proposition. It can demonstrate to potential clients and investors that your business offers something different from your competitors and that you have a clear vision for achieving your goals. Additionally, a well-written company description can help you attract top talent to your business. It can communicate your company's culture, values, and mission, helping you attract employees who share your vision and are passionate about your business's success.

To write an effective company description for your massage therapy business, you must include several key elements. These include your business's history, mission, vision, values, goals, and objectives. Your business's history should provide a brief overview of how it was founded, its growth and development over time, and any significant milestones or achievements. Your mission statement should define the purpose of your business and its overall goals. It should communicate what you hope to achieve with your business and how you plan to do it.

Your vision statement should describe your business's long-term goals and objectives. It should provide a clear picture of what you hope to accomplish in the future and how you plan to get there. Your values should communicate your business's core beliefs and principles. They should provide a framework for decision-making and guide your business's actions and behavior. Your goals and objectives should be specific, measurable, achievable, relevant, and time-bound (SMART). They should provide a clear roadmap for achieving your business's mission and vision.

By including all of these elements in your company description, you can create a comprehensive and effective document that communicates your business's purpose, goals, and values. This will help you attract clients, investors, and employees who share your vision and are passionate about your business's success.

Market Analysis

A market analysis is a crucial component of your massage therapy business plan. It provides an in-depth understanding of your industry, competitors, and target audience. But what exactly is a market analysis, and why is it so essential? A market analysis is an assessment of your industry, including your competitors and target audience. It provides a detailed understanding of the market conditions in which your business operates and helps you identify potential opportunities and threats.

A well-written market analysis is essential for any massage therapy business because it provides critical insights into your industry, competitors, and target audience. It helps you understand the needs and preferences of your clients and provides a framework for developing effective marketing strategies. A market analysis also helps you identify potential opportunities and threats to your business. By understanding your industry and competitors, you can develop strategies to differentiate your business and stand out in a crowded market. Additionally, a market analysis can help you identify potential challenges and risks that may impact your business's success, allowing you to develop strategies to mitigate these risks.

You'll need to include several key elements to conduct a comprehensive market analysis for your business. These include an analysis of your industry, competitors, and target audience. Your industry analysis should provide a detailed overview of the massage therapy industry, including its size, growth trends, and regulatory environment. It should also include information about the different types of massage therapy services available, pricing, and packaging.

Your competitor analysis should provide an in-depth understanding of your competitors, including their strengths, weaknesses, and market share. It should also include an analysis of their marketing strategies and how they target their audience. Your target audience analysis should provide a detailed understanding of your ideal clients, including their needs, preferences, and behaviors. It should also include information about their demographics, psychographics, and purchasing behavior.

By including all of these elements in your market analysis, you can create a comprehensive and effective document that provides a clear understanding of your industry, competitors, and target audience. This will help you develop effective marketing strategies and identify potential opportunities and threats to your business.

Service or Product Line

One of the most critical elements of any massage therapy business plan is the description of your service and product line. This section should provide a detailed overview of your massage therapy services, including pricing and packaging information. A well-written service and product line description is essential for any massage therapy business plan because it provides potential investors, lenders, or partners with a clear understanding of what your business offers. It should communicate your unique value proposition and differentiate your business from competitors. Additionally, a clear service and product line description can help you attract and retain clients by communicating the value and benefits of your services.

To write an effective service and product line description for your massage therapy business plan, you'll need to include several key elements. These include a description of your services, pricing and packaging information, and any additional products or services you offer. Your service description should provide a detailed overview of the massage therapy services you offer. It should communicate the benefits of each service and explain how they meet the needs of your target audience. You may want to include information about the duration of each service, any specialized techniques you use, and any certifications or qualifications you hold.

Your pricing and packaging information should communicate how you price your services and how you package them together. It should include information about the cost of each service, any discounts or promotions you offer, and any additional fees or charges. You may also want to include information about how you accept payment and whether you offer any financing options.

Finally, your additional products and services should

provide a brief overview of any other products or services you offer that complement your massage therapy services. For example, you may offer aromatherapy or retail products that help clients enhance their massage experience. By including all of these elements in your service and product line description, you can create a persuasive document that communicates the value of your services and sets you apart from competitors. This will help you attract and retain clients and position your business for long-term success.

Marketing and Sales

A well-written marketing and sales plan is essential for any massage therapy business plan. This section should outline your strategies for promoting your business, attracting new clients, and growing your revenue. A marketing and sales plan is critical because it helps you identify your target audience and develop strategies to reach them effectively. It also helps you differentiate your business from competitors and communicate your unique value proposition to potential clients. Ultimately, a strong marketing and sales plan can help you attract and retain clients, increase revenue, and position your business for long-term success.

To write an effective marketing and sales plan for your massage therapy business plan, you'll need to include several key elements. These include a description of your target audience, a competitive analysis, marketing strategies, and sales projections.

Your target audience should be clearly defined, including their demographics, psychographics, and any other relevant information. This information will help you develop marketing strategies that resonate with your audience and address their needs and pain points.

Your competitive analysis should provide a detailed overview of your industry and your competitors. It should include information about their strengths, weaknesses, and any opportunities or threats in the marketplace. This information will help you identify areas where you can differentiate your business and develop strategies to compete effectively. Your marketing strategies should outline how you plan to promote your business and attract new clients. This may include a combination of tactics such as social media marketing, content marketing, paid advertising, and referral marketing. Your strategies should be tailored to your target audience and designed to achieve specific goals, such as increasing website traffic or generating new leads.

Finally, your sales projections should provide a detailed analysis of your expected revenue and expenses. This information will help you set realistic goals and develop strategies to achieve them. By including all of these elements in your marketing and sales plan, you can create a compelling document that positions your massage therapy business for long-term success. With a clear understanding of your target audience, competitors, and marketing strategies, you'll be well on your way to achieving your business goals and sharing your passion for healing with others.

Financial Projections

Financial projections are a crucial component of any massage therapy business plan. This section should provide a detailed analysis of your expected revenue, expenses, and profits for the next several years. Financial projections are important because they help you determine whether your business is financially viable and sustainable in the long term. By projecting your revenue and expenses, you can identify potential cash flow issues, estimate your profitability, and determine whether you need to make any changes to your business model or operations.

To create financial projections for your massage therapy business plan, you'll need to start with a detailed analysis of your revenue and expenses. This may include estimating the number of clients you can expect to see each week, the pricing for your services, and any additional sources of revenue you plan to generate (such as retail sales or product offerings). Next, you'll need to estimate your expenses, which may include rent, utilities, supplies, and marketing costs. You'll also need to account for any staffing costs if you plan to hire additional employees.

Once you have a detailed understanding of your revenue and expenses, you can create a projected income statement and cash flow statement. These statements should outline your expected revenue, expenses, and profits for each month or year of operation. It's important to be realistic and conservative when creating financial projections. While it's tempting to project high revenue and low expenses, this can lead to unrealistic expectations and potential cash flow issues down the road. By being conservative in your projections and accounting for potential challenges or unexpected expenses, you can ensure that your business is financially sustainable and set up for long-term success.

Management and Organization

A business plan for a massage therapy business should include a section on management and organization, which outlines the business structure and the roles and responsibilities of key personnel. This section provides a clear understanding of how the business will operate and who will be responsible for each aspect of the operation. Defining the management and organizational structure is important as it ensures that everyone involved in the business is aware of their responsibilities and can work together effectively. It also provides a framework for decision-making, accountability, and delegation of tasks. In the management and organization section of the business plan, you should outline the structure of the business, including the key personnel and their roles and responsibilities. This could include the owner/manager, therapists, receptionists, and any other staff members. It's important to be specific about the duties of each role and how they fit into the overall operation of the business.

You should also outline the management style and communication channels within the business. This could include details on how decisions will be made, how the information will be shared, and how conflicts will be resolved. In addition, you may want to include information on any training or development plans for staff members, as well as succession planning for key positions. Overall, the management and organization section of the business plan is an essential aspect of building a successful massage therapy business. It provides a clear understanding of the structure and responsibilities of the business, enabling effective communication, decision-making, and accountability.

Operations

The operations section of a business plan for a massage therapy instructional business outlines the day-to-day processes and procedures necessary to run a successful business. This section should cover everything from equipment and supplies to scheduling and client communication. Having a detailed operations plan is crucial for any business, especially in the massage therapy industry. This section of the business plan will provide a clear and concise overview of how the business will operate, ensuring that everything runs smoothly and efficiently. It will also help to identify potential issues and areas of improvement, allowing the business to be more proactive in addressing them.

When creating the operations section of a business plan for a massage therapy instructional business, it's important to start by outlining the equipment and supplies necessary to provide quality services. This includes massage tables, linens, oils, and other essential items. It's also important to detail the process for ensuring the cleanliness and sanitation of the equipment and supplies. Next, the operations plan should cover scheduling procedures, including how appointments will be booked, how cancellations and rescheduling will be handled, and how clients will be reminded of their appointments. Communication with clients should also be addressed, including how questions and concerns will be addressed and how feedback will be collected and incorporated.

The operations plan should also include information on the hiring and training process for staff, as well as the process for evaluating employee performance and providing ongoing education and development opportunities. Finally, financial and administrative operations should be covered in the operations section, including how billing and payment will be handled, how taxes will be filed, and how inventory and expenses will be tracked and managed.

Overall, the operations section of a business plan for a massage therapy instructional business should provide a clear and detailed plan for how the business will operate on a day-to-day basis, ensuring that everything runs smoothly and efficiently while providing top-notch services to clients.

SWOT Analysis

What is a SWOT analysis, and why is it important for your massage therapy business? A SWOT analysis is a powerful tool that can help you identify the strengths, weaknesses, opportunities, and threats of your business. By conducting a SWOT analysis, you'll be able to gain a deeper understanding of your business's internal and external factors, which will help you make informed decisions about your future direction.

Let's start with the strengths of your massage therapy business. What sets you apart from your competitors? What are your unique selling points? Perhaps you have a highly trained and skilled team of massage therapists or offer a wide range of specialized massage therapies. Whatever your strengths are, make sure you highlight them in your SWOT analysis.

Now, let's move on to weaknesses. What are the areas in which your business could improve? Perhaps you have a limited marketing budget or struggle to retain clients. It's important to identify your weaknesses so that you can address them and turn them into strengths.

Next, let's look at opportunities. What are the trends and developments in the massage therapy industry that you can take advantage of? Perhaps there is a growing demand for specific types of massage therapies or an untapped market in a particular area. By identifying opportunities, you'll be able to capitalize on them and grow your business.

Finally, let's consider threats. What are the external factors that could potentially harm your business? Perhaps there is increased competition in your area, or changes in regulations could affect your operations. By identifying threats, you'll be able to take proactive steps to mitigate them and protect your business.

In conclusion, conducting a SWOT analysis is crucial in developing a successful massage therapy business. By identifying your strengths, weaknesses, opportunities, and threats, you'll be able to develop a clear strategy for growth and success. So take the time to conduct a thorough SWOT analysis and use it to guide your decision-making process.

Appendices

The appendices section is an important part of a massage therapy business plan that provides additional supporting documents and materials that can help validate and strengthen your plan. This section is where you can include any supplementary information that may not be necessary for the main body of the plan but can provide additional context or support for your ideas.

The appendices section is important because it can help provide a more comprehensive view of your massage therapy business plan. By including supporting documents such as legal agreements, permits, licenses, or relevant research and data, you can provide additional credibility to your plan and demonstrate that you have thoroughly researched and planned your business. Additionally, including relevant material in this section can make it easier for investors or lenders to review and assess your plan.

When compiling your appendices section, make sure to include only relevant and necessary materials. This section should not be used as a catch-all for every document and piece of information related to your business. Rather, focus on including items that can provide additional value to your plan and help to illustrate key points. Some examples of materials that can be included in the appendices section are:

- Resumes and bios of key team members
- Legal agreements and contracts
- Permits and licenses
- Market research and industry data
- Detailed financial projections and statements

- Marketing materials such as brochures or flyers

Make sure to organize your appendices in a clear and concise manner, and reference any items in the main body of the plan as necessary. Keep in mind that while the appendices section is not the main focus of your plan, it can still have a significant impact on how your plan is received and evaluated by investors or lenders.

Crafting a winning business plan for your massage therapy business requires time, research, and attention to detail. But by creating a well-crafted business plan, you'll have a roadmap for success and a clear understanding of what it will take to achieve your goals.

The following is a sample business plan for a massage therapy business located in an all-inclusive resort located in Honolulu, Hawaii:

Executive Summary:

Our massage therapy business, located in an all-inclusive resort in Hawaii, will provide a range of massage and bodywork services to resort guests. With our experienced and skilled therapists, state-of-the-art equipment, and serene environment, we aim to provide our guests with the ultimate relaxation and rejuvenation experience. Our mission is to offer personalized and high-quality services that meet the diverse needs of our guests while ensuring that they have an unforgettable experience.

Company Description:

Our massage therapy business will be located within an all-inclusive resort in Hawaii. The business will provide a range of massage and bodywork services to resort guests, including Swedish massage, deep tissue massage, hot stone massage, aromatherapy massage, and reflexology. Our team of skilled therapists will ensure that our guests receive the highest level of service and care. We will also offer personalized treatments and packages to meet the diverse needs of our guests.

Market Analysis:

The massage therapy industry is growing rapidly in Hawaii, with an estimated annual growth rate of 6.2%. Our target market will primarily consist of resort guests who are seeking relaxation and rejuvenation during their vacation. According to industry research, massage therapy is becoming increasingly popular among travelers, and many are willing to pay a premium for high-quality services. We will also target local residents who are interested in our services.

Service and Product Line:

Our massage therapy business will provide a range of services, including Swedish massage, deep tissue massage, hot stone massage, aromatherapy massage, and reflexology. We will also offer personalized treatments and packages to meet the diverse *needs of our guests. All our services will be provided in a serene and peaceful environment, using state-of-the-art equipment and high-quality products.*

Marketing and Sales Strategies:

We will use a variety of marketing and sales strategies to attract guests to our massage therapy business. Our primary strategy will be to partner with the all-inclusive resort where we are located and promote our services to resort guests through in-room advertising, brochures, and social media. We will also use targeted online advertising and search engine optimization to reach potential guests who are searching for massage therapy services in Hawaii. Additionally, we will offer special promotions and discounts to attract new guests and encourage repeat business.

Financial Projections:

Our massage therapy business is expected to generate revenue of $500,000 in the first year, with a net profit of $100,000. By the third year of operations, we expect to generate revenue of $750,000 and a net profit of $200,000. Our startup costs will include equipment and supplies, staff training, marketing and advertising, and rental fees. We anticipate our revenue will increase steadily as we build our reputation and attract more guests.

Operations:

Our massage therapy business will operate seven days a week, with flexible hours to accommodate the needs of our guests. We will hire a team of skilled therapists who will provide high-quality services to our guests. Our therapists will receive extensive training and ongoing education to ensure they are up-to-date with the latest massage techniques and trends. We will also invest in state-of-the-art equipment and high-quality products to ensure that our guests have the best possible experience.

SWOT Analysis:

Strengths:

• Convenient location within an all-inclusive resort

• Skilled and experienced team of therapists

• Personalized and high-quality services

• Serene and peaceful environment

• State-of-the-art equipment and high-quality products

Weaknesses:

• Limited market reach beyond resort guests and local residents

• Potential challenges with seasonality and fluctuations in demand

Opportunities:

- *Increasing demand for massage therapy services among travelers*
- *Potential to expand services and packages to meet the diverse needs of guests*
- *The growing tourism industry in Hawaii*

Threats:

- *Competition from other massage therapy businesses in Hawaii*

In conclusion, creating a business plan is essential for any massage therapist looking to start their own business. This chapter has provided a comprehensive overview of the key elements of a business plan, including the executive summary, company description, market analysis, service and product line, marketing and sales, financial projections, management and organization, operations, SWOT analysis, and appendices. By including these key sections, you can create a roadmap for your business, define your goals and objectives, and develop strategies for achieving success. Remember, a well-written business plan not only helps you stay focused and on track towards your goals but also provides a solid foundation for attracting investors and securing financing. So, take the time to develop a comprehensive business plan for your massage therapy business, and watch your dreams become a reality.

Chapter Three
Developing Your Brand

Welcome to Chapter 3 of *The Ultimate Guide to Building a Successful Massage Therapy Business*. In this chapter, we'll delve into the world of branding and explore how to develop a strong and effective brand for your massage therapy business.

Your brand is the face of your business, and it's what sets you apart from your competitors. It communicates your values, personality, and purpose to your target audience. A well-crafted brand can help you attract and retain clients, establish trust and credibility, and differentiate your business from others in the industry.

In this chapter, we'll discuss the key elements of successful branding, including a distinctive logo and visual identity, clear and consistent messaging and tone, a compelling brand story, and a strong online presence. We'll also explore how to align your brand with your business goals and values and how to use your brand to create a memorable and engaging client experience.

Whether you're just starting out or looking to rebrand your existing business, this chapter will provide you with the tools and resources you need to develop a strong and effective brand that will set your massage therapy business up for success. So, let's dive in

31

and explore the world of branding!

Successful branding is a critical component of building a successful massage therapy business. Your brand is what distinguishes you from your competitors and creates a connection with your target audience. Your brand encompasses everything from your logo and visual identity to your messaging and tone. It communicates your business's values, purpose, and personality to your customers.

Creating a strong brand is essential for attracting and retaining clients. It helps build trust and credibility with your target audience and can differentiate you from competitors in a crowded marketplace. Your brand also helps you communicate your business's values and purpose, which can be particularly important for attracting clients who share those values.

There are several key elements to creating a successful brand for your massage therapy business. First, you'll need to develop a distinctive logo and visual identity that communicates your brand's personality and values. Next, you'll need to establish clear and consistent messaging and tone that aligns with your brand's purpose and resonates with your target audience. Your brand story is another essential element that communicates the history and values of your business. Finally, a strong and consistent online presence is crucial for reflecting your brand and values across all digital channels. By developing a comprehensive and cohesive brand strategy, you can create a powerful connection with your target audience and build a successful massage therapy business. Let's take a more detailed look at some of the key elements of successful branding, including:

Logo and visual identity

Your logo and visual identity are crucial elements in establishing your massage therapy business's brand. A distinctive and memorable logo can help you stand out in a crowded market and establish a strong visual identity that communicates your brand's personality and values. A strong visual identity can help you create a lasting impression with your clients and potential customers. It can help you establish a sense of trust and credibility, communicate your business's purpose and values, and differentiate yourself from your competitors.

To create a distinctive logo and visual identity, start by identifying your business's key values and personality traits. Use these to inspire your logo design and choose colors, fonts, and imagery that align with your brand's identity. Consider working with a professional designer to ensure your logo and visual identity are professional and high-quality. Once you have established your visual identity, consistently use it across all of your marketing materials, including your website, social media profiles, and printed materials. By creating a strong and consistent visual identity, you can establish a strong brand that communicates your business's values and personality to your clients and potential customers. The following are a few software programs and websites that can be used to create a distinctive logo and visual identity for your business:

- **Canva:** A graphic design platform that allows users to create professional-looking logos and other visuals with customizable templates, fonts, and images.
- **Adobe Illustrator:** A vector graphics editor that provides advanced design tools for creating logos, illustrations, and other graphics.
- **Fiverr:** A freelance marketplace that connects businesses with graphic designers who can create custom logos and visual identity packages.
- **99designs:** A graphic design platform that allows businesses to launch logo design contests and receive submissions from multiple designers.
- **Logojoy:** An online logo maker that uses artificial intelligence to generate unique logo designs based on user preferences and industry trends.
- **Tailor Brands:** An AI-powered branding platform that offers logo design, social media graphics, and other branding tools for small businesses.
- **Wix Logo Maker:** A logo design tool that provides users

with customizable logo templates and design options based on their business type and style preferences.

- **BrandCrowd:** A logo design platform that provides a library of pre-designed logos and branding assets that can be customized to fit a business's unique style and personality.

Canva is a graphic design platform that offers a wide range of tools for creating logos, business cards, social media posts, and other visual elements for your brand. The platform is user-friendly and offers a variety of templates, graphics, and fonts to choose from, making it easy to create a professional-looking logo or visual identity even if you have little to no design experience.

For massage therapy businesses that want to create a more custom logo or visual identity, software programs such as Adobe Illustrator or Photoshop can be used. These programs offer more advanced design tools and allow for greater customization and flexibility. However, they do require a bit more design expertise and may have a steeper learning curve than some of the other options listed.

Overall, many software programs and websites are available for massage therapy businesses to create a distinctive logo and visual identity that communicates their brand's personality and values. By creating a strong brand identity, businesses can establish a connection with their target audience and set themselves apart from competitors.

Messaging and tone

Messaging and tone are crucial components of your brand identity as a massage therapist. Your messaging should convey your business's purpose and values, and your tone should resonate with your target audience. To create a clear and consistent messaging and tone, start by defining your brand's mission, vision, and values. This will help you articulate what you stand for and what sets you apart from your competitors.

Once you have a clear understanding of your brand's purpose and values, you can start crafting messaging that aligns with them. Your messaging should be concise, clear, and focused on the benefits of your massage therapy services. Use language that resonates with your target audience and speaks to their pain points and needs.

Your tone should also be consistent with your brand's purpose and values. If your brand is focused on relaxation and stress relief, your tone should be calming and soothing. If your brand is focused on sports massage and injury recovery, your tone should be more energetic and focused. Here are some more examples of messaging and tone that could align with your brand's purpose and resonate with your target audience:

- **Relaxation and self-care:** "Unwind, rejuvenate, and find your inner peace with our massage therapy services."

- **Pain relief:** "Say goodbye to pain and discomfort. Let us help you feel better and improve your quality of life."

- **Sports massage:** "Train harder, recover faster, and perform better with our sports massage services."

- **Holistic wellness:** "Nurture your body, mind, and spirit with our holistic approach to massage therapy."

- **Luxury and indulgence:** "Experience the ultimate in relaxation and pampering with our luxurious massage services."

- **Health and wellness:** "Invest in your health and well-being with our massage therapy services, designed to promote relaxation and reduce stress."

- **Accessibility and inclusivity:** "We believe that everyone deserves to feel their best. Our massage therapy services are accessible and inclusive to all."

Your tone should also be consistent across all your marketing and branding materials, including your website, social media profiles, and advertising. Remember, your messaging and tone are critical components of your brand identity, and they should be carefully crafted to resonate with your target audience and communicate the unique value of your massage therapy business.

Brand story

Your brand story is a powerful tool that can connect you with your target audience and help you stand out from your competitors. A compelling brand story tells the history of your business and communicates your values and mission to your audience. Your brand story should be authentic, emotional, and engaging and should resonate with your target audience on a personal level. To create a compelling brand story for your massage therapy business, you should start by reflecting on your own journey as a massage therapist. What inspired you to become a massage therapist, and how did you develop your skills and expertise? What are your values and beliefs about the healing power of touch, and how do these inform your approach to your practice?

Next, think about the unique qualities that set your business apart from others in the industry. What makes your massage therapy services unique, and how do you communicate this to your clients? What values and principles guide your business, and how do these translate into the services you offer? Once you have a clear understanding of your own story and the unique qualities of your business, you can begin to craft a compelling brand story that resonates with your target audience. Your brand story should be concise, clear, and emotionally engaging and should be woven into all of your marketing and promotional materials.

Some tips for crafting a compelling brand story include:

1- Starting your brand story with a compelling hook can be an effective way to capture your audience's attention and make a strong emotional connection. For instance, you could start with a statement like "At our massage therapy clinic, we believe that healing begins within," which immediately sets the tone for your brand's mission and values. Or you could share an anecdote about a client who experienced significant pain relief after receiving massage therapy, highlighting the effectiveness of your services and your commitment to helping others.

It's important to choose a hook that is both relevant to your business and resonates with your target audience. This will help draw and invest them in your brand's journey. Additionally, make sure that your hook is authentic and reflects the true essence of your business. This will help build trust and establish a positive reputation in the industry. By starting your brand story with a compelling hook, you can create a powerful emotional connection with your audience and set the stage for a strong and memorable brand narrative.

2- Authenticity is especially important in the massage therapy business, as it involves a high level of trust between the therapist and the client. Clients seek out massage therapy for various reasons, including physical pain relief, stress reduction, and overall well-being. It's important for massage therapists to be transparent about their training and qualifications, as well as the techniques and products used during a session. By being authentic and honest with clients, massage therapists can build trust and establish a strong reputation within the industry. Additionally, being true to their values and beliefs can help massage therapy businesses differentiate themselves from competitors and attract clients who share their values. For example, a massage therapy business that prioritizes eco-friendly and sustainable practices can appeal to clients who prioritize environmentalism in their purchasing decisions. Overall, authenticity is crucial to building a successful massage therapy business that prioritizes trust and client satisfaction.

3- In order to make your brand story compelling, it's essential to focus on emotions. Emotions are what make us human and help us connect with others. By creating a brand story that evokes emotions, you can connect with your audience on a personal level and build a strong relationship with them.

When crafting your brand story, consider the emotions you want to evoke. Do you want to inspire your audience with tales of overcoming adversity? Do you want to make them feel joy and happiness with stories of how your business has helped others? Or do you want to create a sense of trust and security by sharing your business's values and mission?

Whatever emotions you want to evoke, be sure to craft your story accordingly. Use descriptive language and storytelling techniques to paint a picture in your audience's minds and evoke the emotions you want them to feel. Focusing on emotions can make your brand story more memorable, relatable, and impactful.

4- In the massage therapy business, your brand story should communicate the history and values of your business in a way that resonates with your target audience. Starting with a compelling hook can draw in potential clients and make them more interested in learning more about your business. It's important to be authentic in your brand story, communicating the unique qualities and values of your business without trying to be something you're not.

Emotions are a key component of the massage therapy experience, and your brand story should reflect that. Think about the emotions you want your clients to feel when they come to your business, and use your brand story to connect with them on a personal level. For example, you may want to evoke feelings of relaxation, rejuvenation, and well-being.

Visuals can also play an important role in communicating your brand story in the massage therapy business. Consider using photos or videos of your massage space, treatment rooms, or happy clients to help bring your story to life and make it more engaging for potential clients. This can also help to build trust and credibility with your audience, as they can see your business in action and get a sense of what it would be like to receive a massage from you.

5- Consistency is a crucial aspect of branding, and it's essential to maintain a consistent brand story across all your marketing and promotional materials. Your brand story should be an integral part of your overall brand identity and should be reflected in everything you do, from your website design to your social media posts.

When your brand story is consistent, it helps build trust and credibility with your audience. It shows that you are reliable and committed to your brand's values and mission. Consistency also helps your audience recognize and remember your brand, making it more likely that they will choose your services over your competitors.

To ensure consistency in your brand story, it's essential to have a clear understanding of your brand's values, personality, and tone of voice. This will help you create a cohesive brand image that resonates with your target audience. Additionally, you should establish brand guidelines that outline your brand's visual identity, messaging, and tone of voice. These guidelines can be used to ensure consistency across all your marketing and promotional materials.

In the massage therapy business, consistency in your brand story can help establish your credibility as a trustworthy and reliable therapist. It can also help you stand out from the competition and attract more clients to your business. By maintaining consistency in your brand story, you can build a strong and recognizable brand that resonates with your target audience.

By crafting a compelling brand story that communicates the history and values of your business, you can establish a connection with your target audience and build a strong, loyal customer base for your massage therapy business.

Having an Online Presence

In today's digital age, having a strong and consistent online presence is essential for any business, including a massage therapy business. Your online presence should accurately reflect your brand and values across all digital channels, including your website, social media platforms, and online directories. A strong online presence can help you connect with new and existing clients, build trust and credibility, and establish your business as a leader in the industry. It can also help you stay top-of-mind with your audience and drive traffic to your website or physical location.

Develop a website:

In order to create a strong online presence, the first and foremost thing every business should do is to create a website. It serves as a powerful marketing tool that can help you attract new clients and retain existing ones. Your website should accurately reflect your brand and values, be easy to navigate, and provide all the necessary information about your services and pricing. A well-designed website is crucial because it's often the first point of contact for potential clients. In today's digital age, people expect businesses to have a website that they can visit to learn more about their services and pricing. Your website can also help you establish credibility and build trust with your audience. A professional-looking website shows that you are serious about your business and that you are invested in providing quality services to your clients.

When developing your website, it's important to keep your brand and values in mind. Make sure that your website's design, color scheme, and content are consistent with your overall brand image. Use high-quality images and clear, concise language to communicate your services and pricing. Make sure that your website is easy to navigate and that all the important information is easy to find.

Additionally, consider incorporating features such as online booking, customer reviews, and frequently asked questions to make the website user-friendly and informative. Lastly, make sure that your website is mobile-responsive, as more and more people are accessing the internet through their mobile devices. A well-designed and informative website can be a game-changer for your massage therapy business and can help you attract new clients and grow your business. In Chapter 5 of the book, you can find a wealth of detailed information on website building. From selecting the right hosting platform to designing user-friendly interfaces, Chapter 5 provides an in-depth exploration of the key considerations and best practices that will empower you to create a compelling and functional website.

Utilize social media

Social media platforms such as Facebook, Instagram, and Twitter are valuable tools for promoting a massage therapy business. By regularly posting updates and engaging with your audience, you can attract potential clients and establish a strong online presence. Social media platforms offer a low-cost and effective way to market your business, reach a wider audience, and build relationships with potential clients. With billions of active users on various platforms, social media is an essential part of any modern marketing strategy.

To make the most out of social media, start by identifying the platforms your target audience is most active on. Create a business account and fill out all the necessary information, including a profile picture, cover photo, and bio. Then, start posting regular updates about your services, promotions, and events. Engage with your audience by responding to comments and messages, and use relevant hashtags to increase your visibility. Consider using paid advertising on platforms such as Facebook and Instagram to further promote your business. Regularly monitor your analytics to track your progress and make adjustments to your strategy as needed. By using social media effectively, you can increase brand awareness, attract new clients, and build a loyal following for your massage therapy business. Enhance the nuances of different platforms and create different content strategies with the comprehensive guide in Chapter 5.

Claim Your Online Listings

Online directories are websites that allow businesses to create a profile and provide information about their services. These directories can include general websites like Google My Business, Yelp, and TripAdvisor, as well as industry-specific directories. Listing your massage therapy business on online directories can help potential clients find your business easily. When people search for massage therapy services in their area, these directories often appear at the top of the search results. Having a strong presence on these directories can increase your business's visibility and credibility.

To get started with online directories, create a profile on

popular websites like Google My Business, Yelp, and TripAdvisor. Be sure to provide accurate and up-to-date information about your business, including your location, services offered, and contact information. Once your profile is live, encourage satisfied clients to leave reviews, as positive reviews can help improve your business's ranking on these directories. Regularly monitor your listings to ensure that your information is up-to-date and that no negative reviews need to be addressed. By actively managing your online directory presence, you can increase your business's visibility and attract more clients to your massage therapy practice.

Here are some online options that can be used to improve your business's online presence through online directories:

- **Google My Business:** This is a free online directory provided by Google that allows businesses to create a profile, list their services, and share important information such as hours of operation, contact details, and photos. Google My Business listings appear in Google Maps and search results, making it easier for potential clients to find your business online.

- **Yelp:** Yelp is an online directory that provides information about local businesses, including massage therapy businesses. Business owners can claim and update their Yelp listing, respond to customer reviews, and share information about their services and pricing.

- **TripAdvisor:** This online directory primarily focuses on travel-related businesses, including massage therapy businesses catering to tourists or travelers. Claiming and updating your TripAdvisor listing can help potential clients find your business when they are researching massage therapy services in your area.

- **Angi:** A website that allows users to search for and rate businesses in various categories, including massage therapy.

- **HealthProfs:** A directory of health and wellness professionals, including massage therapists, where businesses can create a profile and be found by potential clients.

- **Thumbtack:** A platform where businesses can create a profile and bid on projects or services posted by potential clients in their area.

- **MassageBook:** A directory specifically for massage therapists where businesses can create a profile, manage their schedules, and accept online bookings.

- **WellnessLiving:** A platform that offers a suite of tools for wellness businesses, including a directory for customers to search and book appointments with massage therapists.

These directories can help increase the visibility of your

massage therapy business and attract more clients. To make the most out of online directories, it's important to ensure that all business information is accurate and up-to-date, including contact information, website URL, and business hours. It's also important to monitor and respond to customer reviews and inquiries in a timely and professional manner, as this can significantly impact a business's reputation and online visibility. By utilizing online directories, massage therapy businesses can increase their online presence and attract new clients while also maintaining their reputation and credibility in the industry.

Use consistent branding

Consistency is key when it comes to building a strong and memorable brand for your massage therapy business. One way to ensure consistency is by using the same logo, color scheme, and messaging across all of your digital channels, including your website, social media, and online directories. Using a consistent visual and messaging identity helps to create a cohesive and recognizable brand for your business. This can make it easier for potential clients to identify and remember your business, which can ultimately lead to increased brand awareness and client loyalty.

To ensure consistency across all digital channels, create a style guide outlining your brand's visual and messaging identity. This guide should include your logo, color palette, typography, and messaging guidelines. Use these elements consistently in all digital materials, including your website, social media profiles, online directories, email marketing, and any other digital channels you use to promote your business. For example, if your brand's color scheme is blue and green, make sure these colors are used consistently across all channels. Use the same font and style for your business name and tagline, and ensure that your messaging is consistent in tone and style across all digital platforms.

By maintaining a consistent visual and messaging identity across all digital channels, you can create a strong and memorable brand for your massage therapy business, which can ultimately help attract and retain clients. The following are a few websites that can be used to help create a cohesive and recognizable brand:

- **Canva:** Canva is a graphic design platform that offers pre-made templates and design elements to create a consistent visual brand across all digital channels. It can be used to create logos, social media posts, email newsletters, and other marketing materials.

- **Coolors:** Coolors is a color palette generator that can help you choose and create a consistent color scheme for your brand. It offers customizable palettes, as well as the ability to generate random color schemes for inspiration.

- **Grammarly:** Grammarly is a writing assistant that can help ensure consistent messaging across all digital channels. It checks for grammar, spelling, punctuation errors, and inconsistencies in tone and style.

- **Hootsuite:** Hootsuite is a social media management platform that can help you schedule and post consistent content across all social media channels. It offers features like post-scheduling, analytics, and social listening to help you manage your brand's online presence.

- **Google Analytics:** Google Analytics is a web analytics service that can help you track and analyze user behavior on your website. By analyzing user data, you can ensure that your website and digital channels meet your audience's needs and provide a consistent user experience.

- **Adobe Color:** Adobe Color is a free online tool that allows you to create and save color schemes. You can select a base color and generate complementary, analogous, or monochromatic color schemes that can be used across all digital channels.

- **Google Fonts:** Google Fonts offers a wide range of free fonts that can be used for branding purposes. You can select a font that reflects your brand personality and use it consistently across all digital channels.

- **BrandColors:** BrandColors is a website that offers color codes for popular brand logos. You can use this website to find the exact color codes used by your favorite brands and use them in your own branding materials.

These websites can be used in various ways to create a cohesive and recognizable brand. Canva can be used to design consistent logos and visual elements, while Coolors can help choose a consistent color scheme. Grammarly can ensure consistent messaging across all digital channels, while Hootsuite can help manage and schedule consistent social media content. Google Analytics can help ensure that your website and digital channels are providing a consistent user experience.

Monitor and Respond to Reviews

Online reviews have become an integral part of any business's online presence. They can significantly impact a business's reputation and success, including massage therapy businesses. It is important to monitor and respond to all reviews, whether positive or negative, in a professional and timely manner. Online reviews are often the first point of contact for potential clients when looking for a massage therapist. Positive reviews can help build trust and credibility, while negative reviews can damage a business's reputation. Responding to positive or negative reviews shows that you value your clients' feedback and are committed to providing excellent service.

To effectively monitor and respond to online reviews,

massage therapy businesses can use various online tools and platforms such as Google My Business, Yelp, TripAdvisor, and Facebook. These platforms allow businesses to claim their listings, respond to reviews, and engage with their customers. When responding to reviews, it is important to maintain a professional and positive tone, thank the reviewer for their feedback, and address any specific concerns or issues raised in the review. This can help turn a negative review into a positive experience for the reviewer and potentially attract new clients.

In addition to responding to reviews, massage therapy businesses can also encourage satisfied clients to leave reviews on various platforms to help boost their online presence and reputation. This can be done through various means, such as email requests, social media posts, and in-person reminders.

Several options for managing online reviews may include:

- **Claiming and verifying your business on review sites:** Make sure your business is listed on popular review sites like Yelp, Google, and Facebook and that you've claimed and verified your business on those sites. This will allow you to respond to reviews and update your listing as needed.
- **Monitoring reviews regularly:** Set up alerts to be notified when a new review is posted about your business. This will allow you to respond promptly and professionally to any

feedback, positive or negative.

- **Responding to all reviews:** Take the time to respond to all reviews, both positive and negative. Thank customers for their positive feedback and address any concerns or issues raised in negative reviews. This shows that you value customer feedback and are committed to providing excellent service.

- **Encouraging customers to leave reviews:** Ask satisfied customers to leave a review of your business on review sites or social media platforms. You can do this in person or by sending follow-up emails after appointments.

- **Addressing negative reviews:** If you receive a negative review, it's important to respond quickly and professionally. Apologize for any issues raised and offer a solution or resolution to the customer's concerns. This shows that you are proactive in addressing customer feedback and are committed to improving your business.

To communicate review requests to clients, you can do the following:

1. **Include a review request in follow-up emails:** After a client's appointment, send a follow-up email thanking them for their visit and encouraging them to leave a review of your business.

2. **Provide review site links on your website and social media profiles:** Make it easy for clients to leave a review by including links to popular review sites on your website and social media profiles.

3. **Offer incentives for leaving reviews:** Consider offering a small discount or free service to clients who leave a review of your business. This can encourage more clients to leave feedback and help boost your online reputation.

4. **Ask for reviews in person:** If you have a good relationship with a client, ask them in person if they would be willing to leave a review of your business. This personal touch can be more effective than a generic email request.

Overall, by being proactive and responsive to online reviews and encouraging satisfied clients to leave feedback, you can build a strong online reputation and attract more clients to your massage therapy business.

In conclusion, a strong brand is essential for any business, including massage therapy practices. In this chapter, we have discussed several key elements of brand development that can help set your practice apart from the competition. Starting with your logo and visual identity, it's important to have a recognizable and memorable brand image that accurately reflects your values and mission. Additionally, crafting clear and consistent messaging and tone across all your communication channels helps to establish a cohesive and trustworthy brand image. Furthermore, telling a compelling brand story can help connect with your audience on a personal level, creating a deeper emotional connection that builds lasting relationships.

Having an online presence is crucial for reaching potential clients and building your brand. Developing a user-friendly website, utilizing social media, and claiming your online listings can help increase visibility and improve your chances of being found online. Consistency is key, and using the same branding across all your digital channels helps to create a recognizable and cohesive image. Finally, monitoring and responding to online reviews is essential for building and maintaining a positive reputation. By addressing both positive and negative feedback in a professional and timely manner, you can demonstrate a commitment to providing high-quality service and create a positive impression on potential clients. By implementing these strategies and developing a strong brand image, you can differentiate yourself from competitors and establish a reputable and recognizable massage therapy practice.

Chapter Four

Marketing and Promotion

Welcome to Chapter 4 of *The Ultimate Guide to Building a Successful Massage Therapy Business*! In this chapter, we'll explore the marketing and promotion world. As a massage therapist, you're passionate about helping your clients achieve relaxation, stress relief, and pain reduction. But in order to make your business successful, you need to promote your services effectively and reach new clients. Marketing and promotion can feel overwhelming, but it's essential for building a thriving massage therapy business. In this chapter, we'll break down key marketing strategies and help you develop a marketing plan that aligns with your brand and target audience.

We'll start by exploring referral marketing, which is a powerful tool for leveraging your existing clients to refer new clients to your business. We'll also delve into social media marketing, content marketing, and local marketing strategies that can help you reach potential clients and build your brand. By the end of this chapter, you'll have a comprehensive understanding of effective marketing and promotion strategies for your massage therapy business. So let's dive in and start building your marketing plan for success!

Marketing and promotion are key elements of building a successful massage therapy business. While providing high-quality services is important, letting potential clients know about your business and the services you offer is equally important. This requires identifying the most effective marketing channels for your business and developing a marketing strategy that aligns with your brand values and goals.

To begin developing a marketing strategy, it's important to first identify your target audience and their needs. This will help you understand which marketing channels will be most effective in reaching your potential clients. For example, if your target audience is primarily middle-aged individuals with chronic pain, traditional print advertising may not be the most effective way to reach them. Instead, you may want to focus on building a strong online presence and leveraging social media channels to connect with potential clients.

It's also important to consider how your marketing strategy aligns with your brand values and goals. Your marketing messaging should be consistent with your brand story, tone, and visual identity. This helps to reinforce your brand and build trust with potential clients. Effective marketing and promotion can take many forms, from referral marketing to content marketing to local partnerships and advertising. By identifying the most effective channels for your business and developing a strategy that aligns with your brand, you can effectively promote your massage therapy services and grow your business. You need to identify the most effective marketing channels for your business and create a marketing strategy that aligns with your brand. Key strategies for marketing and promotion include:

Referral Marketing

Referral marketing is a powerful tool for any massage therapy business. It relies on the concept of word-of-mouth advertising, where satisfied clients refer their friends, family, and colleagues to your business. Referral marketing is an effective and low-cost way to grow your client base because it is based on trust and personal relationships. To leverage your existing clients for referral marketing, you need to create a referral program. This program should incentivize your clients to refer others to your business. For example, you could offer a discount or a free session for every new client referred by an existing client.

You can use various channels such as social media, email, and in-person conversations to promote your referral program. Be sure to communicate the program's benefits and how it works to your clients. Encourage them to share their positive experiences with others and provide them with tools such as referral cards or links to your website to make it easier for them to refer others.

When implementing a referral program, it's important to track and measure its success. Use analytics tools to determine how many new clients are coming from referrals and adjust your program accordingly. Referral marketing can be a powerful tool for building a loyal client base and growing your business. By leveraging the power of word-of-mouth advertising, you can tap into a network of satisfied clients who can help spread the word about your services. There are several ways to accomplish referral marketing for your massage therapy business:

- **Incentives:** Offer incentives to your current clients to refer new clients to your business. This can be in the form of discounts, free sessions, or other rewards. Make sure to communicate the incentive clearly to your current clients and track referrals to ensure that rewards are given appropriately.

- **Referral Cards:** Provide your clients with referral cards that they can give to friends and family. These cards should include your business information, contact details, and a special offer or discount for new clients. Encourage your clients to hand out these cards to those who may be interested in your services.

- **Client Testimonials:** Encourage your clients to share their positive experiences with your business through testimonials or reviews. Share these testimonials on your website and social media pages to show potential clients the benefits of your services.

- **Personalized Communication:** Reach out to your clients personally to ask for referrals. This can be through email, phone calls, or in-person conversations. Let them know that you value their business and would appreciate any referrals they can provide.

- **Partner with Local Businesses:** Partner with other local businesses to cross-promote services and offer joint promotions. This can be a great way to reach a new audience and generate referrals from other business owners.

By implementing these referral marketing strategies, you can increase the number of new clients coming to your massage therapy business and build a strong base of loyal customers who are happy to refer their friends and family.

Social Media Marketing

Social media has become an integral part of our daily lives, and it's no surprise that it has also become a powerful tool for businesses to promote their products and services. As a massage therapy business, leveraging social media channels can help you connect with potential clients, increase brand awareness, and ultimately grow your business. Social media platforms like Facebook, Instagram, Twitter, and LinkedIn have billions of active users, making them an ideal place to promote your business. They are cost-effective compared to traditional advertising and allow you to target specific audiences and track your results in real-time. Social media also allows you to engage with your audience, build relationships, and create a sense of community around your brand.

To effectively use social media for your massage therapy business, you first need to identify which platforms your target audience is using. Once you've identified your target audience and chosen your social media channels, you can start creating content that resonates with them. This can include tips for relaxation, self-care, and stress relief, as well as updates on your services, promotions, and events. It's important to maintain a consistent and professional brand image across all social media channels, including using the same logo, color scheme, and messaging. Engaging with your audience through comments, direct messages, and shares can help create a stronger connection and build trust.

You can also use social media advertising to reach a larger audience and promote your services to potential clients who may not have heard of your business before. This can include targeted advertising based on location, interests, and demographics. Here are some popular social media platforms that can be used to promote a massage therapy business:

- **Facebook:** With over 2 billion active users, Facebook is the largest social media platform in the world. It offers businesses the opportunity to create a business page, share content, and connect with potential clients. The platform also provides advanced targeting options for paid advertising, making it an effective tool for reaching specific demographics.

- **Instagram:** Instagram is a visual platform that is great for sharing photos and videos of your massage therapy business. It has over 1.2 billion active users and allows businesses to showcase their services and create a strong visual brand.

- **Twitter:** Twitter is a great platform for engaging with potential clients and building a community around your massage therapy business. It offers businesses the opportunity to share short and concise updates, share links to blog posts and other content, and connect with influencers and industry leaders.

- **LinkedIn:** LinkedIn is a professional networking platform that can be used to connect with other professionals in the massage therapy industry, as well as potential clients. It offers businesses the opportunity to share updates, publish articles, and connect with other professionals in the industry.

- **YouTube:** YouTube is a video-sharing platform that can be used to share educational and promotional videos about your massage therapy business. It has over 2 billion monthly active users and offers businesses the opportunity to create a strong visual presence and connect with potential clients through video content.

The benefits of using social media platforms to promote a massage therapy business include the following:

1. **Increased visibility:** Social media platforms provide businesses with the opportunity to reach a larger audience and increase brand awareness.

2. **Improved engagement:** Social media platforms allow businesses to engage with potential clients in real-time, build relationships, and create a community around their brand.

3. **Cost-effective marketing:** Social media marketing can be a cost-effective way for massage therapy businesses to reach potential clients and promote their services.

4. **Targeted advertising:** Social media platforms offer advanced targeting options for paid advertising, allowing businesses to reach specific demographics and increase the effectiveness of their marketing efforts.

5. **Strong visual presence:** Social media platforms like Instagram and YouTube provide businesses with the opportunity to create a strong visual presence and showcase their services in a creative and engaging way.

Social media can be a powerful tool for promoting your

massage therapy business, but it's important to use it strategically and consistently to see results. By identifying your target audience, creating engaging content, and maintaining a professional brand image, you can connect with potential clients and ultimately grow your business.

Content Marketing

Creating valuable content is an effective way to educate and engage your target audience. By providing relevant and helpful information, you can establish your expertise in the massage therapy industry and build trust with potential clients. Valuable content helps educate your target audience and sets your business apart from competitors. It also has the potential to attract new clients who are searching for information related to massage therapy and wellness.

There are several ways to create valuable content for your target audience. One effective approach is to start a blog on your business website. You can use your blog to share educational articles, tips and tricks for maintaining good health, and other relevant topics related to massage therapy. You can also create educational videos that showcase different massage techniques, demonstrate proper body mechanics, and highlight the benefits of massage therapy. This can be shared on social media, your website, or through email marketing campaigns.

Another approach is to offer educational webinars or

workshops on massage therapy and wellness topics. This can be a great way to attract new clients and establish your business as a leader in the industry. The following are some options for blogging sites and webinar platforms that can be used for in your content marketing effort:

Blogging Sites:

- **WordPress:** This is a popular blogging platform that is free to use and offers a range of customization options for creating a unique blog that aligns with your brand.

- **Medium:** This blogging site allows you to reach a wider audience by posting your content to a larger community. It also provides analytics to help you track your reach and engagement.

- **Squarespace:** This is a website builder that also offers blogging capabilities. It provides visually-appealing templates and is easy to use, making it a great option for those new to blogging.

Webinar Platforms:

- **Zoom:** This platform allows you to host free webinars and online meetings with up to 100 participants. It also provides tools for screen sharing and recording.

- **GoToWebinar:** This platform is designed specifically for hosting webinars and offers features such as polls, surveys, and Q&A sessions to engage your audience.

- **WebinarJam:** This platform provides a range of tools for creating engaging webinars, including customizable landing pages, email automation, and interactive features like live chat and polls.

The benefit of using these types of platforms for content marketing is that they can help you establish your expertise and thought leadership in the massage therapy industry. By creating valuable content that educates and engages your audience, you can attract new clients and build a loyal following. Webinars, in particular, can provide a more interactive and personalized experience for potential clients, allowing you to connect with them on a deeper level.

However, when using these platforms, it's important to ensure that your content is accurate and reflects your brand's values and mission. You should also be mindful of privacy and security concerns, particularly when hosting webinars that may involve sensitive information. Finally, it is important to have a strategy in place for promoting your content and reaching your target audience, as simply creating content may not be enough to generate leads and conversions.

No matter what approach you take, be sure to focus on providing value to your target audience. This will help you establish credibility, build trust, and ultimately drive more business to your massage therapy practice.

Local Marketing

Local marketing is the practice of targeting potential clients in your local area through local events, partnerships, and advertising. By focusing your efforts on your immediate community, you can establish yourself as a trusted and reliable resource for massage therapy services. This can help you build a loyal customer base and generate new business through referrals and word-of-mouth marketing.

Local marketing is important because it allows you to connect with potential clients in your immediate area, who are more likely to become regular customers. By participating in local events and forming partnerships with other businesses in your community, you can establish a presence and build trust with potential clients. This can lead to increased brand awareness, improved reputation, and ultimately more business. There are several ways to implement local marketing strategies for your massage therapy business. Here are a few ideas:

- **Participate in local events:** Look for opportunities to participate in local events, such as health fairs, charity runs, and community festivals. This can help you connect with potential clients and promote your business in a fun and engaging way.

- **Form partnerships with other businesses:** Consider partnering with other businesses in your community, such as gyms, spas, and wellness centers. You could offer special discounts to their clients in exchange for them promoting your services.

- **Advertise in local publications:** Look for local publications, such as newspapers and magazines, and consider placing ads in them. This can help you reach a broader audience and establish yourself as a local expert in massage therapy.

- **Offer referral incentives:** Encourage your existing clients to refer their friends and family to your business by offering them incentives, such as discounts on future services. This can help you generate new business through word-of-mouth marketing.

By implementing local marketing strategies, you can establish yourself as a trusted and reliable resource for massage therapy services in your local community. This can help you build a loyal customer base and ultimately grow your business.

In conclusion, marketing and promotion are essential for building a successful massage therapy business. By utilizing a variety of marketing strategies, such as referral marketing, social media marketing, content marketing, and local marketing, you can reach potential clients and create a strong brand presence in your local community. Referral marketing is a powerful tool for leveraging your existing client base to refer new clients to your business. Social media marketing can help you connect with potential clients, promote your services, and engage with your audience. Content marketing, through blogging and webinars, can educate and engage your target audience, establishing your business as an authority in the field. Finally, local marketing can target potential clients in your local area through events, partnerships, and advertising. By developing a comprehensive marketing strategy, you can attract new clients, establish your brand, and grow your massage therapy business.

Chapter Five
Building a Strong Online Presence

As a massage therapist, building a strong online presence is critical for the success of your business. In today's digital age, having a website and social media presence is essential for connecting with potential clients and promoting your services. In this chapter, we will explore the key strategies for building a strong online presence that aligns with your brand and values. We will discuss the importance of creating a professional and informative website, developing a content strategy that resonates with your target audience, utilizing social media channels to engage with potential clients, and investing in online advertising to expand your reach. By following these strategies, you will be able to build a strong online presence that helps you connect with clients and grow your business.

Business owners cannot ignore the importance of having an online presence in today's digital age. The same goes for massage therapy businesses, which can greatly benefit from a well-crafted online presence. One of the key components of building a strong online presence is creating a website that accurately reflects your brand and values. Your website should be professional, visually appealing, easy to navigate, and provide all the necessary information about your services, pricing, and contact information.

71

This is often the first point of contact for potential clients, so it's important to make a good first impression.

In addition to having a website, utilizing social media and other online platforms can greatly expand your reach and connect you with potential clients. As mentioned in the previous chapter, social media channels such as Facebook, Instagram, and Twitter provide opportunities to engage with your audience, promote your business, and even offer exclusive deals and promotions. Maintaining a consistent and active presence on these platforms can build relationships with your followers and attract new clients. Also, creating valuable content through a blog, videos, or other forms of media is also a great way to engage with your audience and showcase your expertise. By sharing your knowledge and insights, you can establish yourself as a subject matter expert in the field and build trust with potential clients.

Online advertising can be a powerful tool for massage therapists looking to grow their business. It allows them to target specific demographics and geographic areas to ensure their message reaches the right people. Before investing in online advertising, however, it's important to set clear goals and define the target audience. Choosing the right platform, crafting compelling ad copy and visuals, and monitoring and optimizing campaigns are also key strategies for building a strong online presence through online advertising.

Before launching an online advertising campaign, massage therapists should define their goals. This will help them create more effective campaigns and measure their success. The goals might include increasing website traffic, generating leads, or promoting a specific service or product. By having a clear objective in mind, massage therapists can craft targeted ads that resonate with their audience and generate better results.

To build a successful online advertising campaign, it's important to define the target audience based on factors such as age, gender, location, interests, and behaviors. This will help massage therapists create ads that resonate with their audience and generate better results. By understanding their target audience, massage therapists can better tailor their advertising campaigns to meet their needs.

There are many online advertising platforms to choose from, including Google Ads, Facebook Ads, Instagram Ads, and LinkedIn Ads. Each platform has its own strengths and weaknesses, so it's important for massage therapists to choose the platform(s) that best align with their goals and target audience. For example, Facebook Ads might be ideal for targeting local clients, while Google Ads might be better for reaching a wider audience.

Crafting compelling ad copy and visuals is also critical to

building a strong online presence through advertising. The copy and visuals should be aligned with the massage therapist's brand and messaging and should be attention-grabbing to capture the audience's attention. By creating compelling ad copy and visuals, massage therapists can encourage potential clients to click through to their website.

Once the advertising campaigns are launched, monitoring their performance is key to their success. Analytics tools can be used to track metrics such as click-through rates, conversion rates, and cost-per-click. By monitoring the performance of the campaigns, massage therapists can make adjustments as needed to optimize their effectiveness. Overall, by following these key strategies, massage therapists can create effective online advertising campaigns that reach the right people and help them grow their businesses.

When it comes to implementing an online marketing campaign for a massage therapy business, it's important to choose the right person or team for the job. The key concepts that a massage therapy business owner should discuss with a potential online marketing campaign implementer include their experience in the field, their understanding of the business and target audience, their approach to goal-setting and metrics tracking, their familiarity with the various online advertising platforms, their ability to craft compelling ad copy and visuals, and their strategy for optimizing campaigns. It's also important to discuss their communication and reporting process, as well as their availability and responsiveness to feedback and questions. By discussing these key concepts with potential candidates, a massage therapy business owner can make an informed decision and choose an online marketing campaign implementer who can help them build a strong online presence and grow their business.

As a massage therapist, building a strong online presence is essential for the success of your business. In today's digital age, having a website and social media presence is critical for connecting with potential clients and promoting your services. Thus far in this chapter, we have discussed the importance of creating a professional and informative website, developing a content strategy that resonates with your target audience, utilizing social media channels to engage with potential clients, and investing in online advertising to expand your reach. In this section, we will delve deeper into each of these topics, exploring key strategies for building a strong online presence that aligns with your brand and values. By following these strategies, you will be able to build a comprehensive online presence that helps you connect with clients and grow your massage therapy business.

Creating a Professional and Informative Website

Creating a professional and informative website is essential for any massage therapy business looking to establish a strong online presence. Your website is often the first point of contact for potential clients, so it's important to make a good first impression. A well-crafted website can help you showcase your services, pricing, and contact information in a way that resonates with your target audience. So, why is creating a professional website so important for a massage therapy business? The answer lies in the power of first impressions. When a potential client visits your website, they form an impression of your business within seconds. A poorly designed or outdated website can leave a negative impression and turn potential clients away. On the other hand, a professional and informative website can inspire confidence and encourage potential clients to take the next step.

But what does it mean to create a professional and informative website? At its core, a professional website should be visually appealing, easy to navigate, and provide all the necessary information about your services, pricing, and contact information. Your website should reflect your brand and messaging, using colors, fonts, and imagery that are consistent with your business identity. It's important to use high-quality images that showcase your services and create a positive impression. Navigation should be clear and intuitive, with easy-to-find information about your services, pricing, and contact information.

In addition to being visually appealing and easy to navigate, your website should also be informative. Your website is an opportunity to showcase your expertise and experience in the massage therapy field. Consider including information about your training and credentials, as well as any specialized services or techniques you offer. You may also want to include testimonials from satisfied clients, which can help build trust and credibility with potential clients.

So, how can you create a professional and informative website for your business? Start by defining your brand and messaging, and choose a design and layout that reflects that identity. Ensure to include all necessary information about your services, pricing, and contact information, and consider including additional information showcasing your expertise and experience.

Creating a website on your own can be a cost-effective option for business owners with the necessary skills and time to invest in the process. However, to create a website on your own, you will need to have some technical skills, such as an understanding of website design, HTML, CSS, and other programming languages. You will also need creativity and design skills to create a website that is visually appealing and easy to navigate. There are advantages to creating a website on your own, such as the ability to have complete control over the design and functionality of your website, as well as the potential cost savings. Additionally, creating your own website can be a learning experience that allows you to develop new skills and gain a deeper understanding of the technology behind websites. On the other hand, creating a website on your own can be time-consuming and may not result in a professional-looking website if you don't have the necessary skills. Additionally, you may encounter technical challenges or issues that require specialized knowledge to resolve.

When it comes to creating a professional website for your massage therapy business, one of the decisions you'll need to make is whether to create the website in-house or outsource the web design to a professional company. While some businesses may have the skills and resources to create a website on their own, outsourcing your web design can be a smart choice for many reasons. Several benefits to outsourcing your web design include cost savings, convenience, and access to a wide range of design tools and resources. Web design companies often offer competitive pricing and flexible packages, allowing businesses to select a web design package that fits their needs and budget. Let's explore several online options that can be used to develop a website:

- Wix is a popular website builder known for its user-friendly platform and drag-and-drop design tools. Wix offers a range of templates that can be customized to create a professional-looking website without the need for extensive design skills. Wix also offers a range of features such as e-commerce functionality, SEO tools, and social media integration, making it a comprehensive solution for businesses of all sizes.

- Squarespace is another popular website builder that offers sleek and modern templates with a focus on strong visual design and user experience. Squarespace offers a range of customization options, including the ability to add custom CSS and HTML code, making it a flexible platform for businesses with more advanced design needs.

- WordPress is a popular content management system that offers a flexible and customizable platform with a wide range of plugins and themes. WordPress can be used to create a custom website that accurately reflects a massage therapy business's brand and messaging, with the ability to add custom features such as e-commerce functionality, contact forms, and more.

- Weebly is a website builder that offers easy-to-use tools and a range of features, including e-commerce functionality, membership options, and social media integration. Weebly also offers a mobile app that allows business owners to manage their website on-the-go.

- GoDaddy is a website builder that offers website builder

tools and professional design services, with a focus on creating affordable and effective websites for small businesses. GoDaddy offers a range of templates and customization options, as well as SEO tools and social media integration.

- Shopify is an e-commerce platform that offers website builder tools and customizable templates, specifically designed for online stores. Shopify offers a range of features, including product management, inventory tracking, and payment processing, making it a comprehensive solution for businesses that sell products online.

- 99designs is a unique design contest platform that allows businesses to receive multiple design concepts from various designers and choose their favorite. 99designs offers a range of design services, including website design, branding, and marketing materials.

- Web.com offers website design and marketing services specifically for small businesses, with a focus on creating affordable and effective websites. Web.com offers a range of customization options, as well as SEO and marketing services, to help businesses improve their online presence.

- Hibu offers website design and digital marketing services with a focus on helping small businesses improve their online presence. Hibu offers a range of services, including website design, SEO, and social media marketing.

- SiteBuilder is an easy-to-use website builder platform that offers a wide range of templates and customization options. SiteBuilder also offers SEO and social media integration, making it a comprehensive solution for businesses of all sizes.

- Duda offers website builder tools and professional design services with a focus on creating mobile-responsive websites. Duda offers a range of templates, customization options, and SEO and e-commerce functionality.

When selecting a web design company, it is important to consider factors such as their experience and expertise, their portfolio of previous work, their pricing and package options, their communication and project management process, and their reputation in the industry. Look for companies that specialize in designing websites for massage therapy businesses, and ask for references and case studies to ensure they have experience in the field. It's also important to choose a company that communicates clearly and effectively throughout the design process and is willing to work with you to ensure your website accurately reflects your brand and messaging.

Developing a Content Strategy that includes Blog Posts, Videos, and Other Types of Valuable Content

That Resonate with Your Target Audience

Developing a content strategy is an essential part of building a strong online presence for your massage therapy business. In today's digital age, it's not enough to simply have a website and social media presence. To truly connect with potential clients and build a loyal following, businesses need to create valuable and engaging content that resonates with their target audience. This means understanding your audience's needs, interests, and pain points and creating content that addresses those topics in a meaningful way. In this section, we'll explore why developing a content strategy is important, what types of content you should consider creating, and how to create a content strategy that resonates with your target audience. By following these tips and strategies, you'll be able to create valuable content that helps you connect with clients and grow your business.

Blog posts are a powerful tool for massage therapy businesses to connect with their target audience and showcase their expertise. By creating informative and engaging blog content, businesses can establish themselves as thought leader in the field and build trust with potential clients. Also, blog posts can help improve a website's search engine rankings, providing fresh and relevant content that search engines prioritize in their algorithms.

When developing a blog post strategy for a massage therapy

business, it's important to start by identifying the topics that are most relevant and interesting to your target audience. This might include topics related to specific types of massage therapy, tips for maintaining good health, or information on the benefits of massage therapy. Once you have a list of topics, it's important to create a content calendar that outlines the frequency of blog posts and the topics you plan to cover.

When creating blog posts, it's important to consider your target audience's needs and interests. This means writing in a conversational tone, using clear and easy-to-understand language, and providing actionable tips and advice. Additionally, including visuals such as photos or videos can help make blog posts more engaging and visually appealing.

Here are five possible titles for blog posts that a massage therapy business could create:

- **The Benefits of Massage Therapy for Stress Relief** - This blog post could explore the various ways massage therapy can help relieve stress and promote relaxation, providing tips and advice for readers on how to incorporate massage therapy into their self-care routine.

- **Different Types of Massage Therapy and their Benefits** - This blog post could provide an overview of the different types of massage therapy, such as Swedish massage, deep tissue massage, and hot stone massage, and explore the specific benefits of each.

- **Massage Therapy for Athletes: How It Can Improve Performance and Prevent Injury** - This blog post could focus on the benefits of massage therapy for athletes, providing specific examples of how massage therapy can help improve performance, prevent injury, and promote faster recovery.

- **How to Choose the Right Massage Therapist for Your Needs** - This blog post could provide tips and advice for readers on how to find the right massage therapist, including factors to consider, such as experience, qualifications, and pricing.

- **The History of Massage Therapy: How It Evolved Over Time** - This blog post could provide a historical overview of massage therapy, exploring its origins and evolution over time, as well as how it is practiced in different cultures and regions around the world.

To promote blog posts, it's important to share them on social media platforms and include links to the blog on your website. Encouraging readers to share your blog posts on social media can also help increase their reach and visibility. Here are some popular blogging platform options to consider using to promote your massage therapy businesses:

- WordPress is a popular and versatile blogging platform that offers a wide range of customization options and plugins to help enhance your blog. With WordPress, businesses can create a fully customizable blog that reflects their brand and meets their specific needs. Some of the features available include custom themes, widgets, and plugins for things like social media sharing, SEO optimization, and email signups.

- Blogger is a free platform owned by Google that is easy to use and ideal for beginners. With Blogger, businesses can create a simple blog quickly and easily without needing any technical skills or knowledge. The platform provides basic features like customizable themes and easy publishing, making it a great option for businesses that are just getting started with blogging.

- Wix is a website builder that also offers a blog feature, making it a comprehensive solution for businesses. With Wix, businesses can create a professional-looking website and blog all in one place, using the platform's drag-and-drop design tools and customizable templates. Wix also offers a range of features and add-ons, such as social media sharing and email marketing, to help businesses promote their blog and reach a wider audience.

- Medium is a platform that allows businesses to publish blog posts and articles and reach a wider audience. Medium is designed for content creators who want to share their ideas with a larger audience and connect with like-minded individuals. Businesses can use Medium to publish high-quality content, such as thought leadership pieces and industry insights, and reach a wider audience than they might on their own blog.

- Squarespace is a website builder that also offers a blog feature with sleek and modern templates. With Squarespace, businesses can create a visually stunning, easy-to-use and highly functional blog. The platform offers a range of customization options and integrations, such as social media sharing and email marketing, to help businesses promote their blog and engage with their audience.

- Ghost is a platform that focuses on simplicity and ease of use, making it a great option for businesses that want a streamlined blogging experience. With Ghost, businesses can create a simple and elegant blog that is easy to use and highly functional. The platform offers a range of features, such as built-in SEO optimization and social media sharing, to help businesses promote their blog and reach a wider audience.

- Tumblr is a microblogging platform that allows businesses to share short-form content, such as photos, videos, and quotes. With Tumblr, businesses can create a visually stunning blog that is highly shareable and engaging. The platform is ideal for businesses that want to share a mix of content types, from longer-form blog posts to shorter snippets of information.

- Weebly is a website builder that also offers a blog feature with a range of customization options and templates. With Weebly, businesses can create a professional-looking blog that reflects their brand and meets their specific needs. The platform offers a range of features and integrations, such as social media sharing and email marketing, to help businesses promote their blog and reach a wider audience.

It is important to monitor the performance of blog posts using analytics tools. This can help you understand which topics and types of content resonate with your audience, allowing you to refine your content strategy over time. The following are some popular analytic tools that can help with tracking the performance of your blog content:

- **Google Analytics**: A free tool offered by Google that provides detailed insights into website traffic, including metrics such as page views, bounce rate, and average time spent on a page.
- **SEMrush:** A powerful tool that provides in-depth analytics on website traffic, backlinks, and search engine rankings.

- **Ahrefs:** A tool that provides detailed insights into website traffic, backlinks, and keyword rankings, as well as competitor analysis.

- **BuzzSumo:** A tool that helps businesses identify popular content in their industry and track the performance of their own content.

- **Piwik:** An open-source analytics platform that provides detailed insights into website traffic, including real-time data and visitor behavior.

- **Clicky:** A real-time analytics tool that provides detailed insights into website traffic, including heatmaps and visitor behavior.

- **Kissmetrics:** A tool that provides in-depth analytics on website traffic, user behavior, and conversion rates, allowing businesses to optimize their content and website for maximum results.

By using analytics tools to track the performance of your blog content, you can better understand your audience and refine your content strategy to meet your business needs and interests. By using blog posts as part of a broader content strategy, massage therapy businesses can connect with potential clients, establish themselves as thought leaders in the field, and ultimately grow their businesses.

Utilizing Social Media Channels to Engage With Potential Clients and Promote Your Business

What do successful businesses have in common? They know how to utilize social media to engage with potential clients and promote their business. In today's digital age, social media has become essential for building a strong online presence and connecting with customers. But with so many social media channels to choose from, how do you know which ones to focus on and how to use them effectively?

Why should you be utilizing social media to engage with potential clients and promote your massage therapy business? For starters, social media platforms such as Facebook, Instagram, and Twitter provide a direct line of communication between businesses and their target audience. By creating a consistent and active presence on these platforms, massage therapy business owners can engage with potential clients, share valuable content, and promote their services to a wider audience. Additionally, social media can help businesses build relationships with their followers and establish themselves as thought leaders in the industry.

How can you effectively utilize social media to engage with potential clients and promote your massage therapy business? One key strategy is to identify which social media channels your target audience is most active on and focus your efforts on those platforms.

For example, if your target audience is primarily women between the ages of 25-45, you may want to focus on Instagram, which is popular among that demographic. Another important strategy is to maintain a consistent and active presence on social media. This means regularly posting content that resonates with your audience, responding to comments and messages in a timely manner, and engaging with other accounts in your industry.

Creating valuable content, such as educational blog posts or informative videos, is also an effective way to engage with potential clients and promote your massage therapy business on social media. By sharing your knowledge and expertise, you can establish yourself as a trusted authority in the industry and build trust with your audience. Let's explore how some of the more popular social media platforms can be used and their advantages and disadvantages:

- **Facebook:** Facebook is a popular social media platform that can be used by massage therapy businesses to connect with potential clients and promote their services. Advantages include the ability to create a business page, share updates and promotions, and interact with followers through comments and messages. Disadvantages include potential for negative reviews or feedback and limited reach without paid advertising.

- **Instagram:** Instagram is a visual platform that can be used by massage therapy businesses to showcase their services and connect with potential clients. Advantages include sharing high-quality photos and videos, using hashtags to reach a wider audience, and engaging with followers through comments and direct messages. Disadvantages include limited options for clickable links and a focus on visual content over written content.

- **Twitter:** Twitter is a platform that can be used by massage therapy businesses to share updates and engage with potential clients in real time. Advantages include sharing short and concise messages, using hashtags to reach a wider audience, and participating in conversations with followers. Disadvantages include the platform's fast paced nature and limited visual content options.

- **LinkedIn:** LinkedIn is a professional networking platform that can be used by massage therapy businesses to connect with potential clients and other professionals in the industry. Advantages include the ability to create a business page, share updates and articles related to the industry, and network with other professionals. Disadvantages include a smaller audience compared to other platforms and a focus on professional rather than personal content.

- **YouTube:** YouTube is a video-sharing platform that can be used by massage therapy businesses to share educational or promotional videos with potential clients. Advantages include the ability to share longer-form videos and reach a wider audience through search engine optimization. Disadvantages include the time and resources needed to create high-quality videos and the potential for negative comments or feedback.

- **TikTok:** TikTok is a popular platform that can be used by massage therapy businesses to showcase their services and connect with a younger audience. Advantages include sharing short and engaging videos, using hashtags to reach a wider audience, and participating in trending challenges. Disadvantages include a focus on entertaining content over educational content and limited options for clickable links.

- **Pinterest:** Pinterest is a visual platform that can be used by massage therapy businesses to share content related to health and wellness. Advantages include sharing high-quality images and articles, using keywords and hashtags to reach a wider audience, and driving traffic to the business website. Disadvantages include a smaller audience compared to other platforms and limited options for engagement with followers.

Overall, the choice of social media channels will depend on the business's specific goals and target audience. It is important to choose the platforms that align with the brand and values of the business and to maintain a consistent and engaging presence on those platforms.

Utilizing social media channels to engage with potential clients and promote your massage therapy business can be a game-changer for your online presence. By identifying the right platforms for your target audience, maintaining a consistent presence, and creating valuable content, you can build relationships with your followers, establish yourself as an industry leader, and ultimately attract more clients to your business.

Investing In Online Advertising to Reach New Clients and Expand Your Reach

Investing in online advertising can be a powerful tool for massage therapy businesses looking to reach new clients and expand their reach. With the rise of digital marketing, various online advertising platforms are available that allow businesses to create targeted and effective advertising campaigns. By investing in online advertising, massage therapy business owners can increase brand awareness, drive website traffic, and ultimately increase sales.

However, with so many advertising options available, choosing the right platform for your business can be overwhelming. In this section, we will explore the benefits of online advertising and the different platforms available, including Google Ads, Facebook Ads, Instagram Ads, Twitter Ads, and LinkedIn Ads. We will discuss how each platform works, the advantages and disadvantages of each, and how to create an effective advertising campaign that targets your desired audience. By understanding the benefits and nuances of each platform, massage therapy businesses can make informed decisions and maximize their return on investment in online advertising.

Google Ads is an advertising platform offered by Google that allows businesses to create targeted and effective advertising campaigns. Google Ads allows businesses to bid on specific keywords relevant to their business and services. When users search for those keywords on Google, businesses' ads can appear at the top of the search results, increasing the visibility of their services and attracting potential clients.

One of the biggest advantages of Google Ads is its ability to target specific demographics and geographic locations. Businesses can tailor their advertising campaigns to specific audiences, ensuring their message reaches the right people. Additionally, Google Ads provides detailed analytics and reporting, allowing businesses to track the success of their campaigns and adjust their strategies accordingly.

However, there are also some disadvantages to using Google Ads. One of the main drawbacks is the cost. Bidding on popular keywords can be expensive, and businesses need to clearly understand their return on investment to ensure that their advertising spending is worth it. Creating effective ads and targeting the right audience can also be challenging, requiring a good understanding of Google Ads' complex algorithms and analytics.

To create an effective advertising campaign on Google Ads, businesses should start by identifying their target audience and the specific keywords that are relevant to their services. They should then create ads that are visually appealing, concise, and tailored to their audience's needs. Additionally, businesses should continuously monitor their campaigns and adjust their strategies based on the analytics and reporting provided by Google Ads. By consistently refining their campaigns and targeting the right audience, massage therapy businesses can effectively utilize Google Ads to reach new clients and expand their reach. The following are two examples of Google Ads specifically for a massage therapy business:

Example 1:

Headline: Relax and Rejuvenate with Our Massage Therapy Services

Description: Looking for a way to unwind and rejuvenate? Look no further than [Business Name]. Our experienced massage therapists provide a range of services to help you relax and relieve stress. We have everything you need to feel your best, from Swedish and deep tissue massages to aromatherapy and hot stone treatments. Book your appointment today and start feeling the benefits of massage therapy.

Example 2:

Headline: Pain Relief and Wellness Through Massage Therapy

Description: *Tired of living with chronic pain? Want to improve your overall wellness and well-being? [Business Name] can help. Our team of skilled massage therapists specializes in a range of techniques designed to relieve pain and promote healing. From sports massage and trigger point therapy to myofascial release and more, we can help you find the relief you need. Contact us today to book your appointment and start your journey to better health.*

Google Ads can be an effective tool for massage therapy businesses looking to expand their reach and attract new clients. Businesses can tailor their advertising campaigns to reach the right audience by targeting specific demographics and geographic locations. Although there are some disadvantages to using Google Ads, such as the cost and complexity of creating effective ads, businesses can overcome these challenges by continuously refining their campaigns and monitoring the analytics and reporting provided by Google Ads. By following these strategies, massage therapy businesses can utilize Google Ads to promote their services and improve their online visibility. The examples provided demonstrate how massage therapy businesses can create effective ads that resonate with potential clients and highlight the benefits of their services.

Facebook Ads provide businesses with a powerful tool to create targeted and effective advertising campaigns. By selecting their target audience based on demographics, interests, behaviors, and geographic locations, businesses can create ads that appear on Facebook, Instagram, and other partner websites that are part of the Facebook advertising network.

One of the biggest advantages of Facebook Ads is its extensive targeting capabilities, allowing massage therapy businesses to reach a specific audience interested in health and wellness, fitness, and self-care. Furthermore, Facebook Ads are relatively cost-effective, with businesses being able to set their budget and bid for ad placements.

However, there are also some disadvantages to using Facebook Ads. Ad fatigue is one potential issue, as users may become overwhelmed by the amount of advertising content they see on their Facebook feeds. In addition, targeting the wrong audience can result in low engagement and wasted ad spending.

To create an effective advertising campaign on Facebook Ads, massage therapy businesses should begin by identifying their target audience and specific demographics, interests, and behaviors relevant to their services. From there, they can create visually appealing and engaging ads tailored to their audience's needs. It is also essential to monitor campaigns continuously and adjust strategies based on the analytics and reporting provided by Facebook Ads. Overall, Facebook Ads can be a highly effective advertising tool for massage therapy businesses looking to promote their services, specials, and promotions while driving traffic to their website or booking platform.

Instagram Ads is a powerful advertising medium that allows businesses to create visually stunning ads and reach a large audience on one of the most popular social media platforms. Instagram Ads work by allowing businesses to create ads in a variety of formats, such as photo ads, video ads, and carousel ads. Businesses can target specific demographics and interests, ensuring that their ads reach the right audience.

One of the biggest advantages of Instagram Ads is the platform's visual appeal. With its focus on photos and videos, Instagram is an ideal platform for massage therapy businesses to showcase their services and attract potential clients. Additionally, Instagram Ads provide businesses with detailed analytics and reporting, allowing them to track the success of their campaigns and adjust their strategies accordingly.

Nevertheless, there are also some disadvantages to using Instagram Ads. One of the main drawbacks is the competition for attention on the platform, as users are constantly inundated with content. Businesses need to create visually appealing ads that stand out and capture their audience's attention. Additionally, creating effective ads and targeting the right audience can be challenging, requiring a good understanding of Instagram's algorithms and analytics.

To create an effective advertising campaign on Instagram, massage therapy businesses should start by identifying their target audience and the specific demographics and interests relevant to their services. They should then create visually appealing ads that showcase their services and are tailored to their audience's needs. Additionally, businesses should continuously monitor their campaigns and adjust their strategies based on the analytics and reporting provided by Instagram Ads. The following are two examples of effective Instagram Ads specifically for a massage therapy business:

Example 1:

Visual: A photo of a person receiving a massage with a peaceful expression on their face

Caption: Relax and unwind with our massage therapy services. Our experienced therapists will help you relieve stress and rejuvenate your mind and body. Book your appointment today!

Example 2:

Visual: A video showcasing the various massage techniques offered by the business, with calming music in the background

Caption: Whether you need relief from chronic pain or just want to treat yourself to a relaxing massage, we have everything you need. Our skilled therapists offer a range of techniques to meet your needs. Book your appointment now and start feeling the benefits of massage therapy.

By understanding how Instagram Ads work, and the advantages and disadvantages of using this platform, businesses can create effective advertising campaigns that target their ideal clients. Massage therapy business owners can effectively engage with potential clients and increase their brand awareness by utilizing the platform's targeting options, visually appealing content, and analytics tools. However, it's important to keep in mind that Instagram Ads can be costly, and businesses should carefully consider their advertising budget and goals before investing in this platform. With the right strategy and approach, massage therapy businesses can utilize Instagram Ads to effectively promote their services and grow their client base.

Twitter Ads are a powerful tool for businesses to reach a wider audience and promote their services on the popular social media platform. Businesses can connect with potential clients by creating targeted campaigns based on their interests, demographics, and location. One of the biggest advantages of Twitter Ads is its ability to provide businesses with detailed analytics and reporting, allowing them to monitor the success of their campaigns and make necessary adjustments.

However, Twitter Ads also come with certain drawbacks. The limited character count of tweets can make it difficult to create a compelling message that effectively communicates the business's value proposition. Additionally, Twitter's user base tends to be younger, which may not be ideal for businesses targeting older demographics. Despite these challenges, with careful planning and execution, Twitter Ads can be an effective marketing tool for businesses in the massage therapy industry looking to expand their reach and connect with new clients.

Creating a successful advertising campaign on Twitter requires businesses to follow a strategic approach. To begin, businesses need to define their target audience and identify relevant keywords related to their massage therapy services. Once the target audience and keywords are established, businesses need to create visually compelling and engaging ads that convey their message concisely while catering to their audience's needs. It is essential to continuously track the ad campaign's performance and make changes to optimize the campaign's effectiveness based on the insights provided by Twitter Ads' analytics and reporting. By following these steps, businesses can create an effective Twitter ad campaign that helps them reach their ideal audience and expand their client base.

Here are two examples of Twitter Ads specifically for a massage therapy business:

Example 1:

Headline: Relax and Rejuvenate with Our Massage Therapy Services

Description: Looking for a way to unwind and rejuvenate? Look no further than [Business Name]. Our experienced massage therapists provide a range of services to help you relax and relieve stress. Book your appointment today and start feeling the benefits of massage therapy. #relax #massage #wellness

Example 2:

Headline: Pain Relief and Wellness Through Massage Therapy

Description: Tired of living with chronic pain? Want to improve your overall wellness and well-being? [Business Name] can help. Our team of skilled massage therapists specializes in a range of techniques designed to relieve pain and promote healing. Contact us today to book your appointment and start your journey to better health. #painrelief #wellness #massage

Ultimately, Twitter Ads offer a cost-effective and efficient way for massage therapy businesses to reach a wider audience and promote their services. While the limited character count of tweets presents a challenge, businesses can overcome it by creating visually appealing and engaging ads that cater to their audience's needs. By continuously monitoring the campaign's performance and making necessary adjustments, businesses can maximize the campaign's effectiveness and optimize their ad spend. Twitter Ads is a powerful tool that can help massage therapy businesses expand their reach and connect with potential clients.

LinkedIn allows businesses to create targeted and effective advertising campaigns. LinkedIn Ads work by allowing businesses to target specific audiences based on their job titles, company size, industry, and more. When users browse LinkedIn, businesses' ads can appear on their feeds and pages, increasing the visibility of their services and attracting potential clients.

One of the biggest advantages of LinkedIn Ads is its ability to target specific professional demographics, making it an ideal platform for businesses targeting working professionals in specific industries. Additionally, LinkedIn Ads provides detailed analytics and reporting, allowing businesses to track the success of their campaigns and adjust their strategies accordingly. Another advantage is the ability to create sponsored content, such as articles and videos, which can help businesses establish thought leadership

103

and credibility in their industry.

Nevertheless, there are also some disadvantages to using LinkedIn Ads. One of the main drawbacks is the cost, which can be higher than other social media advertising platforms. Additionally, LinkedIn's user base tends to be smaller than other social media platforms, making it less ideal for businesses targeting a wider audience.

Entrepreneurs starting a massage business should identify their target audience and the specific professional demographics relevant to their services before creating an effective LinkedIn Ads campaign. They should then create ads that are visually appealing, concise, and tailored to their audience's needs. Additionally, businesses should continuously monitor their campaigns and adjust their strategies based on the analytics and reporting provided by LinkedIn Ads.

For a massage therapy business, LinkedIn Ads can be an effective advertising tool, as it allows businesses to target professionals who may be in need of massage therapy services to alleviate workplace stress and promote overall wellness. Business owners can utilize LinkedIn Ads to promote their services, specials, and promotions, and drive traffic to their website or booking platform. By consistently refining their campaigns and targeting the right audience, massage therapy businesses can effectively utilize

LinkedIn Ads to reach new clients and expand their reach.

In today's digital age, building a strong online presence is essential for any business looking to succeed. Chapter 5 has provided valuable insights into creating a professional and informative website, developing a content strategy, and utilizing social media channels to engage with potential clients and promote your massage therapy business. Additionally, we explored the benefits of investing in online advertising to reach new clients and expand your reach.

By following the strategies outlined in this chapter, massage therapy entrepreneurs can establish a strong online presence that effectively communicates their brand message, showcases their expertise, and builds trust with their target audience. Through engaging website design, valuable content creation, and targeted advertising, businesses can drive traffic to their website, increase their visibility, and ultimately attract new clients.

However, building a strong online presence is an ongoing process that requires dedication, creativity, and flexibility. As technology and consumer behaviors continue to evolve, businesses must stay ahead of the curve and continuously adapt their strategies to remain relevant and effective. By incorporating the tactics outlined in this chapter and staying up to date with emerging trends and best practices, massage therapy businesses can position themselves for success in the competitive online landscape. With a strong online presence, businesses can build brand awareness, attract new clients, and ultimately achieve their business goals.

Chapter Six

Pricing and Packaging Your Services

As a massage therapist, pricing and packaging your services can be challenging. Determining the right pricing strategy that fits your target audience and differentiates you from your competition is essential. Moreover, creating service packages that meet the diverse needs of your clients while being flexible and affordable is crucial for success. This chapter will focus on pricing and packaging your services to maximize your revenue and build a loyal client base. We will delve into key strategies for pricing and packaging your services, including offering add-on services and providing package deals and discounts. By implementing these strategies, you can increase your revenue and provide added value to your clients. Remember, pricing and packaging your services is essential to building a successful massage therapy business. It's time to take your massage therapy business to the next level and ensure long-term success. Let's get started!

Pricing and packaging your services is an important aspect of building a successful massage therapy business. You need to determine the right pricing strategy for your business, create service packages that meet your clients' needs, and offer add-on services that increase your revenue. You can price and package your services using the following strategies:

107

Determine Your Pricing Strategy Based on Your Target Audience and Your Competition

Determining the right pricing strategy for your massage therapy business is critical to your success. Pricing your services too high can turn away potential clients, while pricing them too low can undervalue your expertise and skills. To determine the best pricing strategy for your business, you need to consider your target audience and your competition. Your pricing strategy should be based on your target audience and your competition. Understanding your target audience's needs, preferences, and willingness to pay can help you determine the optimal price point for your services. Similarly, researching your competitors' pricing can give you insights into the prevailing market rates and help you stay competitive.

Determining your pricing strategy based on your target audience and competition is essential because it allows you to set the right price for your services, attract more clients, and increase your revenue. You can strike the right balance between attracting clients and earning a fair profit by pricing your services appropriately. To determine your pricing strategy, start by researching your target audience's demographics, such as age, gender, income, and location. There are several ways to research your target audience's demographics for a massage therapy business, including:

1. **Online surveys:** Use online survey tools such as SurveyMonkey or Google Forms to gather information from your current clients or potential clients about their demographics and interests.

2. **Social media analytics:** Utilize the analytics tools provided by social media platforms such as Facebook and Instagram to gain insights into the demographics of your followers and engagement rates.

3. **Website analytics:** Analyze your website traffic using tools such as Google Analytics to gain information about your website visitors' demographics, including age, gender, location, and interests.

4. **Local market research:** Conduct research on the local market using tools such as census data or local government records to gain insights into the demographics of the community in which your business operates.

5. **Competitor analysis:** Analyze the demographics of your competitors' customers using customer reviews, social media, and other online sources to gain insights into your target audience's characteristics.

It is also helpful to consider factors such as their lifestyle, preferences, and the value your targeted consumer base place on massage therapy services. This information can help you identify a price point that is appealing to your target audience while also meeting your revenue goals. By utilizing these methods, massage therapy businesses can gain a deeper understanding of their target audience's demographics and tailor their pricing strategies and service packages to meet their clients' needs and preferences.

Next, research your competition to understand their pricing structure, the services they offer, and their target audience. Analyzing their pricing can help you determine the right pricing range for your services and identify opportunities to differentiate your business and offer unique value. Here are some ways to research your competition:

1. **Check their website:** Start by visiting your competitors' websites and look at the services they offer, their pricing structure, and any promotions they may be running. This will help you understand how they position their services and how they differentiate themselves from other massage therapy businesses.

2. **Visit their social media pages:** Take a look at their social media pages, such as Facebook, Instagram, and Twitter. Look at the types of posts they share, how often they post, and how they engage with their followers. This can give you insights into how they build and maintain their online presence, as well as what their audience may be interested

in.

3. **Secret shop:** Consider visiting your competitor's business as a customer. This will allow you to experience their services firsthand and see how they interact with their clients. Take note of their pricing structure and any add-on services they offer. You can also observe the quality of their facilities, the professionalism of their staff, and the overall atmosphere of their business.

4. **Attend industry events:** Attend trade shows, conferences, and other events in the massage therapy industry to connect with other professionals in the field. This can provide you with the opportunity to network, learn about new trends, and gain insights into what your competitors are doing.

5. **Conduct online research:** Use search engines, industry publications, and online directories to find information about your competitors. This can help you identify their strengths and weaknesses, as well as their pricing strategy and target audience.

By conducting thorough research on your competition, you can gain valuable insights that can help you differentiate your massage therapy business and develop a pricing strategy that is competitive and attractive to potential clients. In conclusion, determining the right pricing strategy based on your target audience and competition is crucial to building a successful massage therapy business. By researching your target audience and competition, you can set a competitive price point, attract more clients, and grow your revenue.

Offer Add-On Services, Such as Aromatherapy or Hot Stone Massages

Add-on services are additional services that can be offered in addition to the core massage therapy services. By offering a variety of add-on services, a massage therapy business can cater to the individual needs and preferences of its clients and potentially increase its revenue. Offering add-on services can increase a massage therapy business's revenue by providing clients with additional services that complement their massage therapy sessions. These services can also differentiate a business from its competitors and enhance the overall customer experience.

Examples of add-on services may include the following:

1. **Aromatherapy**: This involves adding essential oils to the massage oil or lotion to enhance the therapeutic effects of the massage. Some common essential oils used in aromatherapy include lavender, peppermint, and eucalyptus.

2. **Hot Stone Massage**: This is a type of massage that uses heated stones to relax muscles and improve circulation. The

stones are usually made of basalt, a type of volcanic rock that retains heat well.

3. **Deep Tissue Massage**: This type of massage focuses on the deeper layers of muscle and connective tissue. It can help relieve chronic pain and improve range of motion.

4. **Reflexology**: This type of massage involves applying pressure to specific points on the feet or hands to stimulate the body's natural healing processes. It can be helpful for reducing stress and promoting relaxation.

5. **Body Scrubs**: This involves using a scrub made from natural ingredients like sugar or salt to exfoliate the skin and remove dead skin cells. It can be helpful for improving the texture and appearance of the skin.

6. **Cupping Therapy**: This involves placing cups on the skin to create suction and promote blood flow. It can help reduce muscle tension and improve circulation.

7. **Stretching**: This involves incorporating stretching exercises into the massage to improve flexibility and range of motion.

To offer add-on services, a massage therapy business must first identify the most popular and relevant add-on services based on the needs and preferences of its target audience. They should also train their massage therapists on how to provide these services effectively and incorporate them into their massage therapy sessions. Additionally, business owners should consider pricing these add-on services appropriately, taking into account the cost of providing the service and the value it provides to the client. By offering well-designed add-on services, a massage therapy business can create a more comprehensive and satisfying experience for its clients and increase its revenue.

Create Service Packages that Meet the Needs of Your Clients and Offer A Range of Options and Prices

Creating service packages that meet the needs of your clients and offer a range of options and prices is an essential component of building a successful massage therapy business. Service packages allow you to offer various options to clients at different price points, increasing the likelihood of repeat business while generating additional income streams.

Creating service packages that meet your clients' needs and offer a range of options and prices can benefit your business in several ways. Firstly, it enables you to cater to the different needs and preferences of your clients, providing them with more options to choose from. Secondly, service packages can help you stand out from your competitors and offer unique value to your clients. Finally, offering service packages can increase the perceived value of your services and encourage clients to book more sessions with you.

To create effective service packages, it is important to understand your clients' needs and preferences. Conduct market research to determine the services and pricing options most appeal to your target audience. Consider offering packages that combine different types of massages or add-on services, such as aromatherapy or hot stone massages. Create packages at different price points to cater to clients with different budgets. Finally, make sure to clearly communicate the benefits and value of each package to clients to encourage them to book. By creating service packages that meet your clients' needs and offer a range of options and prices, you can increase your business's revenue and provide added value to your clients. The following are some examples of service packages:

1. **Relaxation Package**: This package is designed to help clients unwind and de-stress. It includes a 60-minute Swedish massage, aromatherapy, and a soothing scalp massage. This package is ideal for clients who are looking to improve their overall well-being and reduce anxiety.

2. **Pain Relief Package**: This package is focused on relieving chronic pain and tension. It includes a 90-minute deep tissue massage, hot stone therapy, and

cupping. This package is perfect for clients who suffer from chronic pain due to conditions such as arthritis or fibromyalgia.

3. **Sports Massage Package**: This package is tailored to athletes and fitness enthusiasts. It includes a 60-minute sports massage, stretching, and a cooling peppermint foot scrub. This package is ideal for clients who want to improve their performance, prevent injuries, and speed up recovery after workouts.

4. **Couples Massage Package**: This package is designed for couples who want to enjoy a relaxing and intimate experience together. It includes two 60-minute Swedish massages, aromatherapy, and a glass of champagne. This package is perfect for couples celebrating a special occasion or enjoying a romantic getaway.

5. **Prenatal Massage Package**: This package is tailored to expectant mothers who want to relieve stress and discomfort during pregnancy. It includes a 60-minute prenatal massage, gentle stretching, and a calming lavender foot soak. This package is ideal for expectant mothers in their second or third trimester.

6. **Monthly Membership Package**: This package includes a set number of massages per month at a discounted rate. This package is great for clients who need regular

massages to manage chronic pain or stress.

7. **Hot Stone Massage Package**: This package includes a set number of hot stone massage sessions. A hot stone massage uses smooth, heated stones to warm up tight muscles and provide relaxation. It's a great option for clients who enjoy a deeper sense of relaxation.

8. **Aromatherapy Massage Package**: This package includes a set number of aromatherapy massage sessions. Aromatherapy massage incorporates essential oils to enhance the massage experience and promote relaxation and well-being.

The packages can also be priced differently based on the level of service and duration, giving clients the flexibility to choose a package that fits their budget. The following are some package options ideas based on the level of service and duration:

1. **Basic Package**: This package can include a 30-minute massage session at a lower price point for clients who are on a tight budget.

2. **Standard Package**: This package can include a 60-minute massage session at a moderate price point for clients who want a more extensive massage experience.

3. **Premium Package**: This package can include a 90-minute massage session with a hot stone massage add-on

at a higher price point for clients who want a more luxurious and longer massage experience.

4. **Couples Package**: This package can include two 60-minute massage sessions for couples at a discounted price point.

5. **Monthly Membership Package**: This package can include a monthly membership that provides clients with one massage session per month at a reduced price.

Each service package should be designed to meet your target consumer's unique needs and preferences. By offering a range of options at different price points, you can attract clients with different budgets and preferences and increase your revenue potential.

Provide Package Deals and Discounts for Clients Who Book Multiple Sessions or Refer New Clients

Providing package deals and discounts for clients who book multiple sessions or refer new clients is a marketing strategy that can incentivize clients to book more sessions and bring in new business. Offering package deals and discounts can increase client loyalty and retention, as well as encourage clients to refer their friends and family to your business. By providing discounts for bulk sessions or referrals, clients feel valued and are more likely to continue doing business with you.

To implement this strategy, massage therapy businesses can

offer discounts for clients who book multiple sessions upfront or purchase packages of services. This not only encourages clients to commit to more sessions but also helps stabilize revenue for the business. Additionally, business owners can offer referral discounts to clients who refer new business to them. This can be a win-win situation, as the referred client gets a discount, and the referring client gets a discount on their next session as a thank you. To effectively market and communicate these package deals and discounts, businesses can use email marketing, social media, and their website to inform clients about the offers and encourage them to take advantage of them. The following are some examples of package deals and discounts that provide incentives to consumers:

1. Buy a package of five massages and get one free
2. Refer a friend and receive 10% off your next massage
3. Sign up for a monthly subscription and receive 20% off each massage
4. Book three massages in advance and receive a 15% discount
5. Host a massage party with five or more guests and receive a free massage
6. Give a gift card for a massage and receive a discount on your next visit
7. Book a couples massage and receive a discount on a future visit

8.   Purchase a gift certificate for a certain amount and receive a free add-on service

9.   Referral Program Discount: Offer a discount for clients who refer new clients to your business. For example, offer a 10% discount on their next massage session for every new client they refer.

10.   Seasonal Promotion Package: Create a package deal for a specific season or holiday. For example, offer a "Holiday Stress Relief Package" that includes a massage session, aromatherapy, and a free gift.

11.   Monthly Subscription Package: Offer a monthly subscription package for regular clients. For example, offer a package that includes two monthly massage sessions for a discounted price.

12.   Group Package: Offer a package deal for groups or couples. For example, offer a "Couples Massage Package" that includes two massage sessions and a free gift.

13.   Prepaid Package: Offer a discount for clients who prepay for multiple massage sessions. For example, offer a 10% discount for clients who prepay for 5 or more sessions.

14.   VIP Package: Offer a premium package deal for clients who want a luxurious and personalized experience. For example, offer a "VIP Massage Package" that includes a

customized massage session, hot stone massage, aromatherapy, and a complimentary beverage.

Massage therapy businesses can incentivize clients to book multiple sessions, refer new clients, and increase their overall revenue by offering package deals and discounts. It also helps build customer loyalty and a positive reputation for the business.

In conclusion, pricing and packaging your massage therapy services is an essential part of building a successful business. By determining your pricing strategy based on your target audience and competition, offering add-on services, and creating service packages that meet your client's needs, you can differentiate your business and offer unique value. Providing package deals and discounts for clients who book multiple sessions or refer new clients can also help you build client loyalty and increase revenue. By following these key strategies, you can build a successful massage therapy business that meets the needs of your clients and provides you with a fulfilling career.

Chapter Seven
Managing Your Finances

One critical aspect of running a successful business is managing your finances effectively. Chapter 7 focuses on managing your finances and explores the key strategies and practices you need to follow to build a financially sustainable massage therapy business. Managing your finances requires a strong understanding of financial management principles. In this chapter, we'll delve into the key strategies for managing your finances, including understanding your revenue and expenses, creating a budget, managing your expenses, and investing in your business. By following these practices, you can ensure that your massage therapy business remains financially sound, even as you grow and expand your services. As a massage therapist, your expertise lies in providing high-quality services that help your clients feel better and improve their well-being. However, to build a successful business, you also need to be financially savvy and understand the ins and outs of managing your finances. By following the strategies outlined in this chapter, you can build a strong financial foundation for your business and focus on providing exceptional service to your clients. Let's explore several key strategies for managing your finances.

Understanding Your Revenue and Expenses and Tracking Your Financial Performance Over Time

Understanding your revenue and expenses and tracking your financial performance over time is critical for success. Revenue and expenses are the two key components of your financial performance that determine the profitability of your business. By tracking your revenue and expenses, you can identify areas where you are making money and areas where you are spending more than you should. This information can help you make informed decisions about where to invest your money and how to optimize your spending.

To understand your revenue and expenses, start by tracking all income and expenses related to your business. This can include massage sessions, product sales, rent, utilities, marketing expenses, and any other expenses associated with running your business. It is also essential to categorize your income and expenses and create a profit and loss statement. This statement will provide you with an overview of your business's financial performance, including revenue, expenses, and net income.

Here are two examples of a profit and loss statement for a massage therapy business:

Example 1:	Example 2:
Revenue: Massage Therapy Services - $50,000 Add-On Services - $5,000 **Total Revenue: $55,000**	**Revenue:** Massage Therapy Services - $75,000 Add-On Services - $10,000 **Total Revenue: $85,000**

Expenses:	Expenses:
Rent - $12,000	Rent - $15,000
Utilities - $2,500	Utilities - $3,500
Supplies - $3,000	Supplies - $4,500
Equipment Maintenance - $1,500	Equipment Maintenance - $2,500
Marketing - $4,000	Marketing - $7,500
Payroll - $20,000	Payroll - $30,000
Taxes - $2,000	Taxes - $3,000
Total Expenses: $45,000	**Total Expenses: $66,000**
Net Income: $10,000	**Net Income: $19,000**

Tracking your financial performance over time is also important. By comparing your current financial performance with past performance, you can identify trends and make informed decisions about the future of your business. Consider using accounting software or hiring a bookkeeper to help you manage your finances and track your financial performance.

Here are some examples of accounting software programs that can be used by a massage therapy business:

1.   **QuickBooks:** One of the most popular accounting software programs used by small businesses, QuickBooks offers a range of features, including invoicing, expense tracking, and financial reporting.

2.   **Xero:** A cloud-based accounting software program that

offers features such as invoicing, bank reconciliation, and expense tracking.

3. **FreshBooks:** Another cloud-based accounting software program that includes invoicing, time tracking, and project management features.

4. **Wave:** A free accounting software program that offers invoicing, accounting, and receipt scanning features.

5. **Zoho Books:** A cloud-based accounting software program that includes features such as invoicing, expense tracking, and project management.

One alternative to managing your accounting is hiring a professional bookkeeper to handle it for you. A bookkeeper can handle tasks such as tracking income and expenses, managing accounts payable and receivable, reconciling bank statements, and preparing financial reports. Hiring a bookkeeper can save time and reduce stress for business owners who may not have the expertise or time to handle financial tasks on their own. A bookkeeper can also help ensure that financial records are accurate and up-to-date, which is crucial for making informed business decisions.

When hiring a bookkeeper, it's important to look for someone with experience in small business accounting, as well as knowledge of any specific regulations or tax requirements for massage therapy businesses. Selecting the right bookkeeper is a crucial step in managing the finances of your massage therapy business. To begin, creating a list of potential candidates is important by asking for referrals from other business owners, searching online, or contacting professional organizations. Once you have a list of potential candidates, it is important to conduct interviews to evaluate their experience, qualifications, and communication skills. During the interview, ask about their experience with bookkeeping software, understanding of tax laws, and familiarity with massage therapy businesses. It is also important to verify their credentials and check references to ensure that they have a track record of providing reliable and accurate bookkeeping services. In addition, it is important to evaluate their fees and determine if they are affordable for your business. Overall, selecting a bookkeeper is a critical step in managing your business's financial health, and conducting thorough research and interviews will help you find the best fit for your needs.

Creating A Budget That Includes All of Your Expenses and Revenue Streams

Creating a budget is essential to managing your finances for a successful business. A budget is a financial plan that outlines your expected revenue and expenses over a specific period, typically a year. By creating a budget, you can forecast your business's financial performance, identify potential problems before they arise, and make informed decisions about spending and investment.

Creating a budget is important for several reasons. First, it helps you plan for the future and make informed decisions about your business's financial health. Second, it enables you to manage your expenses and cash flow effectively, which is essential for staying afloat in the long term. Finally, a budget helps you track your progress toward your financial goals, whether that's paying off debt, investing in new equipment, or saving for a rainy day.

To create a budget, start by listing all of your expected revenue streams, such as massage sessions, product sales, or gift certificate sales. Next, list all of your expected expenses, such as rent, utilities, insurance, supplies, and marketing. Be sure to include both fixed expenses, such as rent, that don't change month to month, and variable expenses, such as supplies that may fluctuate. Once you have a comprehensive list of your revenue and expenses, you can use a spreadsheet or budgeting software to track your cash flow and adjust your spending as needed. It's also important to review your budget regularly, ideally monthly, to ensure that you're staying on track and progressing toward your financial goals.

Here are two examples of budget items for a massage therapy business:

Budget 1:	Budget 2 :

Expenses:	Expenses:
Rent: $1,000	Rent: $1,200
Utilities: $300	Utilities: $350
Massage supplies: $500	Massage supplies: $600
Marketing: $200	Marketing: $250
Insurance: $150	Insurance: $200
Equipment maintenance: $100	Equipment maintenance: $150
Total expenses: $2,250	Professional development: $500
	Total expenses: $3,250
Revenue:	**Revenue:**
Massage sessions: $4,000	Massage sessions: $5,000
Package deals: $1,500	Package deals: $2,000
Add-on services: $500	Add-on services: $750
Total revenue: $6,000	Total revenue: $7,750
Profit :	**Profit:**
$6,000 (revenue) - $2,250 (expenses) = $3,750	$7,750 (revenue) - $3,250 (expenses) = $4,500

Owners may opt to operate their businesses without a budget. Running a business without having a budget can lead to significant disadvantages. Without a budget, tracking your expenses and revenue streams can be challenging, making it difficult to make informed financial decisions. This can result in overspending, running out of money unexpectedly, or missing out on opportunities to invest in your business. For example, if you do not have a budget, you may not realize that you are spending too much money on supplies or marketing, which can lead to financial strain. Additionally, without a budget, it can be challenging to plan for unexpected expenses, such as equipment repairs or professional development opportunities, which can put a strain on your finances. In short, not having a budget can lead to financial instability and make it difficult to build a successful massage therapy business.

Managing Your Expenses by Reducing Costs Where Possible and Optimizing Your Spending

Managing expenses by reducing costs and optimizing spending is an important aspect of managing the finances of a business. It involves critically examining all expenses and finding ways to cut costs while maintaining quality service and efficiency. Managing expenses helps to increase profitability and cash flow, which are essential for the growth and sustainability of a massage therapy business. By reducing unnecessary expenses and optimizing spending, a business can free up more resources to invest in areas that drive growth and expansion.

There are many ways to reduce costs where possible and optimize your spending. This could be achieved by negotiating with vendors for better prices, saving on utilities and supplies, and minimizing waste. Another way to manage expenses is to review your spending regularly to identify areas where you can cut back.

For example, you could analyze your marketing expenses to see which channels are most effective and focus your efforts there. Additionally, you could consider outsourcing tasks or using technology to automate processes, which can save you time and money in the long run. By reducing costs and optimizing your spending, you can maximize your profitability and ensure the long-term success of your massage therapy business.

To manage expenses effectively, a massage therapy entrepreneur should start by thoroughly reviewing all expenses, including fixed costs like rent and utilities, as well as variable costs like supplies and marketing expenses. After identifying areas where costs can be reduced, the business should develop a plan for implementing these changes. This may involve negotiating with suppliers, finding cheaper alternatives for supplies, and reducing marketing expenses.

Let's dive deeper into some of the typical expenses associated with a massage therapy business and explore ideas for reducing those expenses:

1. **Rent:** Rent can be a significant expense for a massage therapy business, especially if you have a large space or a prime location. To reduce this expense, consider sharing a space with another massage therapist, subleasing a space, or negotiating a lower rent with your

landlord.

2. **Utilities:** Utilities such as electricity, water, and gas can also be a significant expense. Consider reducing these expenses by using energy-efficient equipment and appliances, turning off lights and equipment when not in use, and negotiating lower utility rates with your providers.

3. **Supplies:** Supplies such as massage oils, linens, and other products can add up quickly. Consider purchasing supplies in bulk, using eco-friendly products, and negotiating with suppliers for better prices.

4. **Equipment:** Equipment such as massage tables, chairs, and other tools can be a significant investment. Consider purchasing used equipment or leasing equipment to reduce costs.

5. **Marketing:** Marketing can be an essential expense for a massage therapy business to attract new clients. Consider cost-effective marketing strategies such as social media and email marketing, including word-of-mouth referrals.

6. **Insurance:** Insurance is a necessary expense to protect your business and yourself as a massage therapist. Consider shopping around for insurance providers to find the best rates and coverage for your business.

7.   **Continuing Education:** Continuing education is crucial for maintaining your massage therapy license and staying up-to-date on industry trends and techniques. Consider taking online courses or attending local workshops to reduce costs.

By carefully managing your expenses and seeking out cost-saving opportunities, you can reduce your overhead and increase your profitability as a massage therapist. Additionally, it is important to regularly review and track expenses to ensure that the business stays within budget and progresses toward financial goals.

Investing In Your Business by Setting Aside Funds For Marketing, Equipment, and Professional Development

Investing in your massage therapy business is crucial for long-term success. By setting aside funds for marketing, equipment, and professional development, you can improve your services and attract more clients. Investing in your business can help you stand out from the competition and build a strong reputation in the industry. By improving your services and staying up-to-date with industry trends, you can provide better value to your clients and increase your revenue.

Marketing is an essential aspect of investing in your massage therapy business. One of the ways to invest in marketing is to hire a professional marketing agency or freelancer. They can help you create a marketing strategy that is tailored to your business and target audience. A marketing strategy can include several components, such as identifying your target market, developing messaging that speaks to your ideal clients, and identifying the best channels to reach them.

Another aspect of marketing your massage business is advertising. You can utilize different advertising channels to reach your potential clients, including social media, email marketing, and local advertising. Social media platforms like Facebook and Instagram can effectively promote your business and engage with potential clients. Email marketing is another effective way to stay in touch with your clients and provide them with valuable information about your business. Local advertising can include print ads in local newspapers, magazines, or flyers. You can also consider sponsoring local events or offering promotional deals to incentivize new clients to try your services.

Investing in marketing can be a significant expense for your business, but it can also be a crucial investment that can help you attract new clients, build your brand, and grow your business. By working with professionals, developing a comprehensive strategy, and utilizing a range of advertising channels, you can effectively market your massage therapy business and set yourself up for long-term success.

Investing in high-quality equipment can significantly improve the client experience and help you work more efficiently, ultimately leading to higher revenue and growth for your business. For massage therapy equipment purchases, you should take your clients' needs into consideration as well as the services you provide. For example, if you offer prenatal massages, you may need a specially designed table to accommodate pregnant women.

To finance the purchase of equipment, consider options such as financing or leasing. Financing allows you to make monthly payments over a period of time, while leasing allows you to rent the equipment for a set amount of time. It is important to carefully review the terms and conditions of these agreements and ensure that they align with your financial goals and budget. Investing in high-quality equipment can also have long-term benefits, such as reducing the need for frequent repairs or replacements. Regular maintenance and cleaning of equipment can also extend its lifespan and ensure optimal performance, ultimately saving you money in the long run.

There are several options for purchasing massage therapy equipment, including online retailers, specialty stores, and even second-hand marketplaces. Popular online retailers such as Amazon and Massage Warehouse offer a wide range of massage tables, chairs, and other equipment from various brands. Specialty stores such as Oakworks and Earthlite also offer high-quality massage equipment. Additionally, second-hand marketplaces such as Craigslist and Facebook Marketplace may have used equipment available for purchase at a lower cost.

Professional development is an important aspect of building and growing a successful massage therapy business. Attending industry conferences, workshops, and continuing education courses can help you stay current with the latest massage therapy techniques and trends and improve the quality of services you offer to your clients. Keeping up with industry advancements and trends is crucial for staying competitive in the massage therapy industry. It can also help you attract new and retain existing clients by offering new and improved services that meet their changing needs.

Research and attend industry conferences and workshops to learn about new massage techniques and trends. Consider taking continuing education courses to improve your skills and knowledge. Networking with other professionals in the industry can also provide valuable opportunities for learning and growth. Finally, make sure to implement what you have learned in your business to improve the quality of services you offer to your clients.

In conclusion, managing your finances is an essential aspect of building a successful massage therapy business. This involves understanding your revenue and expenses, creating a budget that includes all of your expenses and revenue streams, and tracking your financial performance over time. By managing your expenses, reducing costs where possible, and optimizing your spending, you can maximize your profits and invest in your business's growth. This includes setting aside funds for marketing, equipment, and professional development. By implementing these strategies, you can improve the quality of services you offer to your clients and increase your credibility in the industry.

Chapter Eight

Hiring and Managing Employees

As your massage therapy business grows, you may find yourself needing to bring on additional team members to help manage your workload. However, knowing when and how to hire employees can be daunting, and managing a team effectively can be a challenge in its own right. In this chapter, we will explore the key strategies for hiring and managing employees, including understanding the legal requirements, developing job descriptions, screening candidates, providing ongoing training and support, and fostering a positive work environment. By implementing these strategies, you can build a successful team that supports your business's growth and meets your client's needs. So, let's dive into the world of hiring and team management and learn how to build a strong and successful team for your massage therapy business.

Understanding the Legal Requirements for Hiring and Managing Employees

As a massage therapy business owner, understanding the legal requirements for hiring and managing employees is essential for avoiding legal issues and ensuring compliance with employment laws. Not only can legal issues be costly and time-consuming, but they can also damage your business's reputation and hinder its growth. By understanding the legal requirements for hiring and managing employees, you can create a legally compliant and positive work environment for your team. To ensure compliance with employment laws, it is important to understand the following legal requirements for hiring and managing employees:

1. **Equal Employment Opportunity (EEO):** Discrimination based on a person's race, color, religion, sex, national origin, age, disability, or genetic information is prohibited by law. As an employer, it is essential to ensure that your hiring and employment practices comply with EEO laws. To avoid any legal complications, it is necessary to establish policies and procedures that promote equal employment opportunities, regardless of any personal characteristics.

2. **Fair Labor Standards Act (FLSA):** The FLSA sets minimum wage and overtime pay standards, record-keeping requirements, and youth employment regulations. As an employer, you must ensure that you pay your employees at least the minimum wage and overtime pay if they work more than 40 hours per week. It is also crucial to maintain accurate records of employees' hours worked and wages paid to avoid legal violations.

3. **Occupational Safety and Health Act (OSHA):** This

law mandates that employers provide their employees a safe and healthy work environment. Employers must identify and eliminate hazards that could cause harm to their workers and ensure that employees have access to appropriate safety equipment and training. By following OSHA standards and guidelines, employers can prevent accidents, injuries, and illnesses in the workplace.

4.   **Employee Retirement Income Security Act (ERISA):** If you offer an employee benefit plan, such as a retirement plan, you must comply with ERISA regulations, which govern the administration of employee benefit plans. ERISA establishes minimum plan participation, vesting, benefit accrual, and funding standards. Employers must ensure that they follow ERISA guidelines to avoid any legal liabilities.

5.   **Family and Medical Leave Act (FMLA):** This law requires employers to provide eligible employees with up to 12 weeks of unpaid leave per year for certain medical and family reasons. Employers must comply with FMLA regulations, which include providing employees with job protection and maintaining their health benefits during their leave. By adhering to FMLA guidelines, employers can support their employees' health and well-being while fulfilling their legal

obligations.

6.   **Immigration Reform and Control Act (IRCA):** As an employer, you must ensure that your employees are authorized to work in the United States. IRCA requires employers to verify the identity and employment eligibility of all employees.

7.   **Uniformed Services Employment and Reemployment Rights Act (USERRA):** This law protects the job rights of individuals who serve in the military. Employers are required to reemploy service members who return from active duty in a timely and non-discriminatory manner.

8.   **Workers' Compensation:** Most states require employers to provide workers' compensation insurance to employees who are injured on the job. As an employer, you must ensure that you have the necessary insurance coverage and comply with reporting and record-keeping requirements.

9.   **Employee Privacy:** You must ensure that you respect the privacy of your employees and comply with applicable laws regarding employee privacy. This may include protecting personal information, monitoring employee communications, and conducting background checks only in compliance with the law.

To ensure compliance with these legal requirements, it is

essential to consult with an employment lawyer or HR professional who can provide guidance and support. Additionally, it is important to keep accurate records of your hiring and employment practices to demonstrate compliance if necessary.

In summary, understanding the legal requirements for hiring and managing employees is essential for avoiding legal issues, ensuring compliance with employment laws, and creating a positive work environment for your team. By staying informed and seeking professional guidance, you can create a successful and legally compliant massage therapy business.

Developing a Job Description and Screening Candidates to Find the Right Fit For Your Business

When it comes to running a massage therapy business, there are two main options to consider: operating as a solo entrepreneur or scaling your business with employees. Operating as a solo entrepreneur offers the advantage of complete control over your business, allowing you to make all the decisions and keep all the profits. However, it also means that you are responsible for all aspects of the business, including marketing, client management, and administrative tasks, which can become overwhelming and limit your growth potential.

On the other hand, scaling your business with employees allows you to delegate tasks and expand your client base, ultimately increasing your revenue potential. However, this option requires careful planning and management to ensure the business operates smoothly and efficiently. It's important to weigh the pros and cons of each option and determine which is the best fit for your personal and professional goals. If there is a desire to scale your business and possibly open multiple locations, it is necessary to explore the option of hiring employees. The employees needed for a small to midsize massage therapy business may vary depending on the size of the business and its specific needs, but some common roles include:

1. **Massage Therapists**: These are the core employees of a massage therapy business. They provide massage therapy services to clients and are responsible for ensuring that clients have a positive and relaxing experience. When hiring massage therapists, it's important to look for individuals who are licensed and certified in massage therapy and have experience in the industry.

2. **Receptionist/Administrative Assistant**: This employee is responsible for managing the front desk, greeting clients, answering phone calls, scheduling appointments, and managing paperwork. They are often the first point of contact for clients and are responsible for creating a positive and welcoming environment.

3. **Marketing Coordinator**: This employee is responsible for managing the marketing efforts of the business, including developing marketing strategies, creating advertising campaigns, managing social media accounts, and analyzing marketing data. They work closely with the owner to develop a marketing plan that aligns with the business's goals and objectives.

4. **Accountant/Bookkeeper**: This employee is responsible for managing the financial records of the business, including invoicing, billing, payroll, and tax preparation. They ensure the business is financially stable and compliant with all financial regulations.

5. **Cleaning Staff**: This employee is responsible for maintaining a clean and hygienic environment for clients and employees. They are responsible for cleaning massage rooms, bathrooms, and other areas of the business.

6. **Business Development Manager**: This employee is responsible for developing new business opportunities and partnerships. They identify new markets, establish relationships with potential clients, and create marketing materials to attract new business.

Overall, these employees work together to ensure that the massage therapy business runs smoothly and provides high-quality services to clients.

It is important to have a job description in place before hiring employees to clearly define the roles and responsibilities for each position. Developing a job description and screening candidates to find the right fit for your business is crucial for hiring the right employees. A well-written job description will help you attract candidates who have the right skills, experience, and qualifications for the job. When creating job descriptions, it's important to gather information from a variety of sources to ensure accuracy and completeness. Sources may include industry-specific job boards, professional associations, government websites, and O*NET. O*NET is an online database of occupational information. O*NET can be a particularly useful resource as it provides detailed information on the knowledge, skills, and abilities required for specific jobs and information on the tasks, work activities, and work context associated with those jobs. To develop a job description, start by identifying the key responsibilities and qualifications required for the position. Be specific and include any necessary certifications or licenses. Also, consider the qualities and values that are important for your business, such as strong communication skills, a positive attitude, or a commitment to customer service. There are other sources that can help you create effective job descriptions for business, including:

1. **Professional organizations**: Look to organizations like the American Massage Therapy Association or the Associated Bodywork & Massage Professionals for guidance on creating job descriptions specific to the massage therapy industry.

2. **Job description templates**: There are many websites and resources that offer free job description templates you can use as a starting point, such as Indeed, Monster, and LinkedIn.

3. **Competitor job postings**: Check out job postings from competitors in your area to see how they structure their job descriptions and what qualifications they require.

4. **Industry-specific job boards**: Consider posting your job opening on industry-specific job boards, like MassageJobs.com or MassageTherapy.com, to attract candidates with relevant experience.

5. **HR consulting firms**: If you need additional guidance on creating job descriptions, consider hiring an HR consulting firm that specializes in the massage therapy industry. They can provide expert advice and tailor job descriptions to your specific business needs.

By utilizing these sources, you can ensure that your job descriptions accurately reflect the requirements and responsibilities of each position in your massage therapy business. By developing a clear job description and carefully screening candidates, you can find the right fit for your massage therapy business and set your employees up for success.

Once you have a job description, you can begin screening candidates. Screening candidates will ensure that you find the best fit for your business, leading to better job performance, higher employee satisfaction, and, ultimately, a more successful massage therapy business. Start by reviewing resumes and cover letters to identify those who meet the minimum requirements. Then, conduct phone or in-person interviews to further assess their qualifications and fit for your business. Consider using behavioral interview questions to gain insight into how the candidate handles specific situations or challenges. During the interview process, it's important to communicate your company's values and culture to ensure the candidate aligns with your business goals. Consider inviting top candidates for a working interview, where they can observe or participate in a massage therapy session to better understand the job. Here are some interview questions that could be useful for finding the right fit for your massage therapy business:

- What inspired you to pursue a career in massage therapy, and what do you find most rewarding about this profession?
- How do you approach assessing a client's needs and tailoring a massage session to meet those needs?

- How do you prioritize your workload and ensure all clients receive the attention they need and deserve?

- How do you maintain a professional demeanor and ensure clients feel comfortable and respected during massage sessions?

- Can you describe a time when you had to handle a difficult or challenging client and how you managed the situation?

- How do you stay up-to-date with the latest massage therapy techniques and trends, and how do you incorporate this knowledge into your practice?

- How do you handle conflicts or disagreements with colleagues or supervisors, and what strategies do you use to maintain positive working relationships?

- Can you describe a time when you had to adapt your massage technique or approach to meet the needs of a client with specific health concerns or limitations?

- How do you approach marketing yourself and your services to potential clients, and what strategies have you found to be most effective?

- How do you prioritize self-care and avoid burnout in your work as a massage therapist?

- What do you know about our company, and why would you be a good fit for our team?

- Describe a difficult situation you encountered in a previous job and how you resolved it.

- How do you handle conflicts with coworkers or clients?

- Can you give an example of a successful project you have completed in the past?

- How do you stay organized and manage your time effectively?

- Are you comfortable working in a fast-paced environment with multiple priorities?

- How do you handle stressful situations, such as a high volume of clients or unexpected changes to your schedule?

- What are your long-term career goals, and how do you see yourself contributing to our company's growth and success?

It's important to note that these are just a few examples, and you may want to tailor your interview questions to the specific needs and culture of your massage therapy business.

Checking references and conducting background checks is an essential step in the hiring process to ensure that the candidate is a good fit for your business. By checking references, you can learn more about the candidate's past work experiences and performance, as well as their strengths and weaknesses. This information can help you make an informed decision about whether or not to hire the candidate. Background checks are also important to ensure that the candidate has a history of good behavior and is a trustworthy and reliable individual. A background check can reveal any criminal history or other red flags that may indicate that the candidate is not a good fit for your business. However, it's important to note that background checks must be conducted in compliance with federal and state laws, and you should consult with a legal professional before conducting any background checks. Sources for checking references and conducting background checks include but are not limited to:

1. **Previous employers:** Contacting the candidate's previous employers can provide valuable insight into their work performance and behavior.

2. **Professional associations:** If the candidate is a professional association member, you may be able to contact the organization to learn more about their qualifications and reputation.

3. **Personal references:** Asking for personal references can give you a sense of the candidate's character and work ethic outside of their professional experience.

4. **Background check companies:** There are many companies that specialize in conducting background checks. These companies can provide a variety of information, including criminal history, credit history, and employment verification.

5. **Online search engines and social media:** Conducting a

simple online search or checking the candidate's social media profiles can reveal information about their online behavior and public reputation.

It's important to note that background checks must be conducted in compliance with federal and state laws, and you should consult with a legal professional before conducting any background checks. Additionally, you should always obtain the candidate's consent before conducting a background check and provide them with a copy of the report if it is used in the hiring decision. When checking references and conducting background checks, it's important to be respectful of the candidate's privacy and to only ask for information that is relevant to the job. You should also inform the candidate that you will be conducting these checks and obtain their consent before proceeding.

Careful consideration must be taken when recruiting and hiring workers. Hiring the wrong employee can significantly impact your massage therapy business. A bad employee can cause a variety of problems, including decreased productivity, low morale, decreased customer satisfaction, and damage to your reputation. A bad employee may also create a negative work environment that can lead to high turnover rates and difficulty in attracting and retaining high-quality employees. Additionally, a bad employee can be costly in terms of time and money spent on recruitment, training, and

150

potentially legal issues if the employee violates company policies or engages in unethical behavior. Therefore, taking the time and effort to carefully screen and hire the right employees for your business to avoid these negative consequences is important. Taking these steps and being mindful of bad employees can help ensure that you hire the right candidate for your massage therapy business and create a positive and productive work environment for your team.

Provide Ongoing Training and Support to Help Your Employees Succeed

Providing ongoing training and support to your employees is crucial to their success and the success of your business. Investing in your employees through training and development opportunities not only helps them grow in their roles but also shows that you value their contributions and are committed to their professional growth. Ongoing training and support can increase job satisfaction, motivation, and retention rates. Employees who feel valued and supported are more likely to be engaged in their work, take pride in their accomplishments, and contribute to the growth and success of the business. Moreover, investing in employee training can also result in increased efficiency, productivity, and profitability for the business.

There are several ways to provide ongoing training and support for your employees. These include offering in-house training sessions, providing access to online courses and resources, attending industry conferences and workshops, and offering mentorship or coaching opportunities. The following are some examples of ongoing training and support that can help your massage therapy employees succeed:

1. **Continuing Education Courses:** Continuing education courses provide opportunities for employees to learn new massage therapy techniques and stay up-to-date with the latest industry trends. Consider offering to pay for a portion or all of the costs associated with attending these courses.

2. **On-The-Job Training:** Provide your employees with on-the-job training and feedback to help them improve their skills and better meet your clients' needs. This can include regular performance evaluations, peer-to-peer coaching, and mentoring programs.

3. **Professional Development Workshops:** Host or encourage your employees to attend professional development workshops that focus on soft skills, such as communication, leadership, and time management. These skills are essential for building strong relationships with clients and improving overall productivity.

4. **Cross-Training Opportunities:** Consider cross-

training your employees to work in different areas of your massage therapy business. This can help improve their versatility and ensure that your business continues to run smoothly even if one team member is absent. For example, if you have a receptionist who also knows how to perform massage therapy, they can step in and help out if one of your massage therapists is sick or on vacation. This can help prevent cancellations and keep your business running smoothly. Similarly, if you have a massage therapist who is also trained in aromatherapy or other alternative therapies, they can offer those services to clients and potentially increase your revenue streams. By providing cross-training opportunities, you can also improve employee engagement and job satisfaction, as they will have the opportunity to learn new skills and take on new challenges.

By providing ongoing training and support, you can help your employees improve their skills, boost their confidence, and ultimately provide better services to your clients. This can lead to increased customer satisfaction, improved business performance, and a more positive work environment for everyone involved. However, it is important to assess the individual needs and interests of your employees and tailor training opportunities to their specific roles and responsibilities. Regularly checking in with your employees and providing feedback can also help them grow and develop in their roles. Remember, investing in your employees is an investment in the future success of your business.

Creating A Positive and Supportive Work Environment That Encourages Collaboration and Innovation

What makes a great workplace? Is it the pay and benefits, the physical space, or the people you work with? While all of these factors are important, creating a positive and supportive work environment goes beyond just the basics. It's about creating a culture that fosters collaboration, innovation, and a sense of purpose for your employees. When your employees feel valued and supported, they are more likely to be productive and engaged in their work.

So, how can you create a positive and supportive work environment in your massage therapy business? Start by defining your company values and mission and ensure that everyone on your team understands and embodies them. Encourage open communication and feedback and create opportunities for collaboration and team-building activities. Recognize and reward your employees for their hard work and achievements, and provide professional growth and development opportunities. Another important aspect of creating a positive and supportive work environment is ensuring that your physical space is comfortable, clean, and inviting. Make sure your employees have the tools and resources they need to do their job effectively and consider investing in amenities like comfortable seating, natural light, and plants. In summary, creating a positive and supportive work environment is essential for the success of your massage therapy business. By fostering collaboration, innovation, and a sense of purpose, you can create a workplace culture that attracts and retains top talent and helps your business thrive.

In conclusion, hiring and managing employees is a critical component of building a successful massage therapy business. To do this effectively, you must understand the legal requirements for hiring and managing employees, develop a job description, screen candidates to find the right fit, provide ongoing training and support, and create a positive and supportive work environment that encourages collaboration and innovation. By being proactive in your hiring practices and taking steps to avoid hiring employees who may not fit your business culture, you can protect your business and create a positive and productive work environment for your team. By following these strategies, you can attract and retain top talent, foster a culture of growth and development, and ultimately achieve success in your massage therapy business. Remember that building a great team takes time and effort, but the rewards are well worth it.

Chapter Nine

Managing Client Relationships

Building strong relationships with clients is crucial for the success of a massage therapy business. As a massage therapist, you should strive to provide exceptional services that meet the needs of your clients. To achieve this, it is important to create a welcoming and comfortable environment that puts your clients at ease. This includes having a clean and well-maintained workspace, using quality equipment, and playing calming music or using aromatherapy to enhance the experience. Listening to your clients' concerns and providing personalized services is also important. Take the time to ask questions about their health, preferences, and expectations to tailor your services accordingly.

Communication is key to managing client relationships. Clearly and effectively communicate with your clients to ensure they understand your services and prices. It is important to be transparent about your policies, such as your cancellation policy and payment methods. Handling client complaints and concerns in a professional and courteous manner is also crucial. It's important to actively listen to their concerns, apologize for any mistakes or miscommunications, and find a solution that meets their needs. By following these key strategies for managing client relationships, you can build a loyal customer base and create a successful massage therapy business. Let's explore several key strategies for managing client relationships.

Create a Welcoming and Comfortable Environment That Puts Your Clients at Ease

Creating a welcoming and comfortable environment is essential to creating a successful massage therapy business. Clients come to you seeking relaxation and relief, so creating an atmosphere that puts them at ease is important. This can be achieved through various means, such as creating a calm and soothing color scheme, providing comfortable seating and decor, and playing soft, relaxing music. A welcoming and comfortable environment can make a huge difference in how your clients perceive your business. By creating a space that puts them at ease, you can help them relax and feel more comfortable during their massage. This can lead to better results, as clients are more likely to let go of tension and stress when they feel comfortable and relaxed.

To create a welcoming and comfortable environment, consider the following:

1. The colors we surround ourselves with can have a significant impact on our moods and emotions. Choosing soothing colors such as blues, greens, and purples can help create a peaceful atmosphere in your massage therapy business. Blue is often associated with calmness

and serenity, while green is associated with nature and relaxation. Purple is often associated with luxury and can create a sense of comfort and relaxation. Additionally, using neutral colors like beige and cream can create a sense of warmth and tranquility. It's important to consider the impact of color when designing your massage therapy business and to choose colors that will help your clients feel more relaxed and comfortable.

2.   Providing comfortable seating is an essential element of creating a welcoming and relaxing atmosphere in your massage therapy business. When clients come in for a massage, they want to be able to fully relax and let go of any tension or stress they may be experiencing. Uncomfortable seating can be a major hindrance to achieving this goal. Therefore, it's important to invest in comfortable seating options that offer sufficient support and cushioning. This could include a variety of options, such as chairs, couches, or even massage chairs. Massage chairs, in particular, can be a great option as they offer clients the opportunity to fully recline and receive a more immersive massage experience. By providing comfortable seating options, you can enhance your clients' overall experience and ensure they leave feeling refreshed and rejuvenated.

3.   Adding calming decor can be an effective way to enhance the overall ambiance of your massage therapy business. Plants, for example, can add a touch of natural beauty and tranquility to your space while also providing some additional health benefits. Studies have shown that plants can help reduce stress and anxiety and even improve air quality. Water features, such as fountains or indoor waterfalls, can also help create a sense of calm and relaxation. The sound of running water can be soothing and therapeutic, and the visual appeal of a water feature can add a sense of peacefulness to your space. When selecting decor for your massage therapy business, it's important to choose items that are visually appealing and serve a functional purpose in creating a calm and inviting atmosphere for your clients.

4.   Soft lighting is an important aspect of creating a relaxing environment in your massage therapy business. Bright or harsh lighting can be jarring and disruptive to the senses and can detract from the overall experience of your clients. Consider using soft lighting options such as dimmer switches, candles, or lamps to create a calming atmosphere. These can be adjusted to create a more subdued and peaceful light that can help your clients feel more relaxed and comfortable during their visit. You

may also want to consider the placement of your lighting fixtures, as well as the type of bulbs you use, to ensure that the lighting is gentle and soothing. With the right lighting, you can help create a tranquil atmosphere that promotes relaxation and rejuvenation for your clients.

5.   Playing relaxing music is a great way to help your clients unwind and relax during their massage sessions. Calming music has been shown to reduce stress and anxiety levels and promote feelings of relaxation and tranquility. Consider playing soft instrumental music or sounds of nature, such as ocean waves or rainfall. It's important to keep in mind that not all clients may enjoy the same type of music, so it's a good idea to have a variety of options available. You can also ask your clients if they have any music preferences before their session begins. Additionally, be mindful of the volume of the music and ensure that it is not too loud or distracting during the massage session.

Overall, your clients should feel relaxed and at ease from the moment they walk through the door. By taking the time to create a tranquil atmosphere, you can help your clients feel more comfortable and enhance their overall massage experience. This can lead to increased client loyalty and positive word-of-mouth referrals, ultimately contributing to the growth of your business. A welcoming environment can also help to ease any nervousness or anxiety that new clients may feel when visiting your business for the first time. By providing a peaceful and inviting atmosphere, you can create a space where your clients can fully relax and enjoy the benefits of your massage services.

Listen to Your Clients' Concerns and Provide Personalized Services That Meet Their Needs

What sets a successful massage therapy business apart from the rest is its ability to listen to its clients' concerns and provide personalized services that meet the unique needs of the client. Every client is different, and each client may have specific requirements when it comes to massage therapy. Therefore, listening carefully to their concerns and needs and tailoring your services accordingly is essential.

The primary reason for listening to your clients' concerns is to provide them with the best possible massage therapy experience. By taking the time to listen to their needs, you can ensure that your services meet their unique requirements. This can result in a higher level of satisfaction and a more positive experience, which can lead to repeat business and referrals. Additionally, listening to your clients can help you identify areas of improvement and refine your services over time, leading to increased success and growth for your business.

To provide personalized services, you need to take the time to understand your clients' concerns and needs. This can be achieved by conducting a thorough consultation before each massage session to gather information about their physical health, lifestyle, and preferences. During the consultation, ask open-ended questions and listen carefully to their responses. Use their answers to tailor your services to their specific needs, such as focusing on certain areas of the body or using a specific massage technique.

Another way to provide personalized services is to offer a range of massage techniques and modalities. Not every client will have the same needs or preferences, so offering a variety of services can ensure that you have options to meet their individual needs. Additionally, consider providing add-ons or enhancements to your massage services, such as aromatherapy or hot stone treatments, to further customize the experience for your clients.

In summary, listening to your clients' concerns and providing personalized services that meet their needs is critical for building a successful massage therapy business. By taking the time to understand your clients' unique requirements and tailoring your services accordingly, you can create a positive and memorable experience that keeps them coming back for more.

Communicating Clearly and Effectively With Your Clients To Ensure They Understand Your Services and

Prices

Communicating clearly and effectively with your clients is an essential aspect of running a successful massage therapy business. This includes ensuring that your clients understand your services and prices. Clear communication can help build trust with your clients and ensure that they have a positive experience at your business. It can also prevent misunderstandings and conflicts related to pricing or scrvices.

To effectively communicate with your clients, using clear and concise language is important. Use plain language to explain your services and pricing, avoiding jargon or technical terms that may confuse clients. Be transparent about your pricing structure and any additional fees or charges. Consider providing written materials or a brochure that outlines your services and pricing. Listen actively to your clients' questions or concerns and address them in a patient and professional manner. It's also important to be responsive to your clients' communication preferences, whether in-person, over the phone, or via email. By communicating clearly and effectively with your clients, you can build trust and loyalty and ensure thcy have a positive experience at your massage therapy business.

Handling Client Complaints and Concerns In A Professional And Courteous Manner

Handling client complaints and concerns in a professional and courteous manner is a crucial part of running a successful massage therapy business. It's important to address any issues that arise promptly and effectively to ensure that your clients are satisfied and happy with your services. Client complaints can significantly impact your business, both in terms of reputation and financial stability. Ignoring complaints or handling them poorly can lead to negative reviews, loss of clients, and a damaged reputation. On the other hand, handling complaints effectively can lead to increased customer loyalty, positive reviews, and a stronger reputation.

The following are key strategies for handling client complaints and concerns professionally and courteously:

1. **Stay calm and composed:** It's important to remain calm and composed when handling client complaints and concerns. This can help defuse the situation and show the client that you are taking their concerns seriously.

2. **Listen actively:** Listen carefully to your client's complaint or concern without interrupting. This can help them feel heard and validated.

3. **Acknowledge their feelings:** Let your client know that you understand their frustration or disappointment. This can help build rapport and show them that you care about

their experience.

4. **Apologize if necessary:** If the situation calls for it, offer a sincere apology to your client. This can show them that you take responsibility for any mistakes or issues.

5. **Offer solutions:** Work with your client to find a solution that addresses their concern or complaint. This can help resolve the issue and prevent it from happening again in the future.

6. **Follow up:** After resolving the issue, follow up with your client to ensure they are satisfied with the outcome. This can help maintain a positive relationship and show them you value their business.

By following these strategies, you can effectively handle client complaints and concerns in a professional and courteous manner and maintain a positive reputation for your massage therapy business.

In conclusion, managing client relationships is critical for any successful massage therapy business. Creating a welcoming and comfortable environment can help your clients feel at ease and enhance their overall massage experience. Listening to your clients' concerns and providing personalized services that meet their needs is essential in building strong relationships. Effective communication with your clients is crucial to ensuring they understand your services and prices. Additionally, handling client complaints and concerns in a professional and courteous manner is critical to maintaining positive relationships and resolving issues. By following these key strategies, you can build and maintain strong client relationships that are essential to the success of your massage therapy business.

Chapter Ten

Providing High-Quality Services

As a massage therapist, your clients trust you with their well-being and relaxation. To build a successful massage therapy business, providing high-quality services that exceed your clients' expectations is essential. Chapter 10 of The Ultimate Guide to Building a Successful Massage Therapy Business focuses on providing high-quality services, including understanding the basics of massage therapy, customizing services to meet clients' needs, creating a comfortable environment, and continuing professional development. By mastering these key strategies, you can build a loyal client base and establish yourself as a reputable and skilled massage therapist. In this chapter, we'll explore these strategies in depth and provide actionable tips to help you deliver exceptional services to your clients. So let's dive in and learn how to provide your clients the best possible massage experience.

Providing high-quality services is the cornerstone of any successful business. You need to understand the basics of massage therapy, deliver exceptional services that meet the needs of your clients, and continue your education and professional development. Our next step is to better understand several key strategies for delivering high-quality services.

Understanding The Various Types of Massage

167

Therapy and Their Benefits

What is massage therapy, and what are the various types of massage therapy? Massage therapy is a hands-on technique that involves applying pressure and movement to the body's soft tissues. This can be done through a variety of techniques, including rubbing, kneading, tapping, and vibration. Massage therapy is the manipulation of soft tissues in the body, including muscles, tendons, ligaments, and fascia, to improve a person's health and well-being. It is an ancient practice used for centuries to help relieve pain, reduce stress, and promote relaxation. The benefits of massage therapy go beyond just relaxation and stress relief. It has been shown to improve circulation, reduce inflammation, and even boost the immune system.

There are many different types of massage therapy, each with its own unique benefits. Some of the most popular types of massage therapy include:

Swedish Massage

Swedish massage is one of the most popular types of massage therapy, known for its gentle and relaxing techniques. It involves using long, smooth strokes, kneading, and circular movements to ease muscle tension and improve blood flow. The therapist may also use techniques like tapping, vibration, and stretching to enhance the overall effect.

Swedish massage is an ideal choice for those who are new to massage therapy or who prefer a more gentle touch. It can be particularly effective in promoting relaxation, reducing stress and anxiety, and improving overall well-being. In addition, it can help to ease muscle pain and tension, increase the range of motion, and improve circulation throughout the body. Swedish massage can be a wonderful way to unwind, destress, and promote better health and wellness.

Deep Tissue

Deep tissue massage is a type of massage that involves applying sustained pressure using slow, deep strokes and friction across the muscle fibers. It focuses on targeting the deeper layers of muscle and connective tissue, which can be helpful in treating chronic muscle pain and injury. The massage therapist may use their fingers, hands, forearms, and elbows to apply pressure and work on the tight and painful areas of the body.

Deep tissue massage is often recommended for people with chronic pain, limited mobility, or injuries affecting the muscles, tendons, and ligaments. It can also help to improve posture and flexibility, increase range of motion, and promote relaxation. However, it is important to note that deep tissue massage may not be suitable for everyone, and it can be uncomfortable or painful if not done correctly. Therefore, it is essential to communicate with your massage therapist throughout the session to ensure that the pressure and intensity are suitable for your body and preferences.

Sports Massage

Sports massage is a specialized type of massage therapy that is tailored to meet the needs of athletes and those who engage in regular physical activity. It focuses on preventing and treating injuries, as well as enhancing athletic performance. This type of massage typically involves a combination of techniques, such as deep tissue massage, stretching, and compression, to help alleviate muscle tension, reduce soreness, and increase flexibility. Sports massage can be beneficial for athletes of all levels and types of sports, from professional athletes to weekend warriors. It can help to improve the range of motion, increase circulation, and reduce the risk of injury. Sports massage therapists typically have specialized training in anatomy, sports medicine, and kinesiology to provide effective treatment and care for athletes.

Trigger Point

Trigger point massage is a type of massage therapy that targets specific areas of muscle tension, called trigger points, which are commonly associated with chronic pain and headaches. These trigger points are typically small areas of tightness within a larger muscle group and can cause pain, discomfort, and even weakness in the affected area.

During a trigger point massage, the massage therapist applies pressure to the trigger point to release the tension and alleviate pain. This pressure can be applied using various techniques, such as deep tissue massage, myofascial release, and stretching. The pressure can sometimes be uncomfortable, but it should never be painful.

Trigger point massage is often used in conjunction with other massage techniques to provide relief from chronic pain and muscle tension. It is important to communicate with your massage therapist about any discomfort you may feel during the massage and your specific areas of pain or tension. Regular trigger point massage can improve your range of motion, reduce pain and discomfort, and enjoy an overall sense of well-being.

Shiatsu Massage

Shiatsu massage is a popular type of massage therapy that originated in Japan. This technique involves using finger pressure to apply to specific points on the body, known as acupressure points. Shiatsu massage is often used to help alleviate stress and tension and promote overall relaxation.

During a shiatsu massage, the therapist will use their fingers, thumbs, palms, and sometimes even their elbows or knees to apply pressure to specific points on the body. These points are believed to be connected to the body's energy pathways, and by applying

171

pressure to them, the therapist can help to restore balance and promote healing.

Shiatsu massage is often performed on a mat or futon on the floor, and the client typically wears loose, comfortable clothing. The therapist may also incorporate stretching or gentle movements into the massage to help increase flexibility and relieve tension in the muscles.

Overall, shiatsu massage can be a highly effective form of therapy for those looking to reduce stress and tension, improve their overall health and well-being, and promote relaxation.

Thai Massage

Thai massage is a unique type of massage that is often referred to as "lazy man's yoga." It is an ancient healing system that combines acupressure, Indian Ayurvedic principles, and assisted yoga postures to provide a therapeutic and relaxing experience. The massage therapist uses their hands, feet, knees, and elbows to apply pressure to the muscles and stretch the body in various ways, helping to improve flexibility, balance, and circulation. Thai massage is often performed on a mat on the floor, and clients are typically fully clothed. This type of massage can be helpful in reducing stress and anxiety, as well as promoting a sense of calm and relaxation. It can also effectively treat chronic pain and improve range of motion. Overall, Thai massage is a unique and effective form of massage therapy that can benefit the body and mind.

Hot Stone Massage

The hot stone massage is a therapeutic massage technique that incorporates the use of smooth, heated stones, usually made of basalt, a type of volcanic rock that retains heat well. The stones are typically placed on specific areas of the body, such as the back, legs, or hands, and are used to apply pressure and heat to the muscles, promoting relaxation and loosening of tight muscles. The warmth of the stones can also help to increase circulation and blood flow, which can aid in the healing process. The hot stone massage is often used in conjunction with other massage techniques, such as Swedish massage, deep tissue massage, or reflexology, to enhance their therapeutic benefits. It is a popular choice for those seeking a soothing and relaxing massage experience, and it can be especially beneficial for those with chronic pain or tension in the muscles.

Aromatherapy Massage

An aromatherapy massage is a popular type of massage that combines the benefits of massage therapy with the use of essential oils. The oils are extracted from plants and are known for their therapeutic properties, such as promoting relaxation, reducing stress, and improving mood. During an aromatherapy massage, the massage therapist will use different essential oils depending on the client's needs and preferences. The oils are usually diluted with a carrier oil and applied to the skin through massage techniques. The scents of the oils can also be inhaled through a diffuser, creating a calming and soothing environment. Aromatherapy massage can be a great way to enhance massage therapy's benefits, helping promote both physical and emotional relaxation.

Reflexology

Reflexology is a unique type of massage therapy that involves applying pressure to specific areas of the hands and feet, known as reflex points. These reflex points are believed to correspond to different organs and systems in the body, and applying pressure to them can help to improve circulation, reduce stress, and promote overall well-being.

During a reflexology session, the therapist will apply pressure to different reflex points using their fingers, thumbs, and other tools. This pressure can be firm or gentle, depending on the needs of the client. Reflexology is a non-invasive therapy that can be done with the client fully clothed and without the use of oils or lotions.

Reflexology is often used as a complementary therapy to traditional medical treatments and can be helpful in treating a variety of conditions, including headaches, anxiety, and digestive issues. Many people find reflexology to be a relaxing and therapeutic experience that can help them to feel more balanced and centered.

Prenatal massage

Prenatal massage is a type of massage therapy that is specifically tailored to meet the needs of pregnant women. It is designed to help relieve some of the discomforts associated with pregnancy, such as back pain, headaches, and swelling. Prenatal massage is typically performed with the woman lying on her side, using pillows and cushions for support and comfort. The massage therapist will use gentle techniques, such as light kneading and long strokes, to help promote relaxation and ease tension in the muscles. Pregnant women need to choose a massage therapist who is trained and experienced in prenatal massage, as certain techniques and pressure points should be avoided during pregnancy. Prenatal massage can be a safe and effective way to help women manage the physical and emotional challenges of pregnancy.

Chair Massage

Chair massage is a type of massage that is typically done in a seated position, with the client fully clothed and leaning forward into a specially designed massage chair. It is often used in workplace settings or at events where clients may not have the time or privacy for a traditional table massage. Chair massage typically focuses on the neck, shoulders, back, and arms and can be done in as little as 15 minutes. It can help reduce muscle tension, improve circulation, and promote relaxation, making it a convenient and accessible option for those in need of a quick massage.

Craniosacral Therapy Massage

Craniosacral therapy massage is a therapeutic touch that focuses on the craniosacral system, including the skull, spine, and pelvis. This type of massage involves light touches and gentle manipulations of the craniosacral system's bones, tissues, and fluids. This massage aims to help balance the flow of cerebrospinal fluid and promote relaxation, relieve pain, and improve overall well-being. Craniosacral therapy massage is often used to treat a variety of conditions, including migraines, chronic pain, anxiety, and depression. It can also be helpful for people recovering from injuries or surgeries. Craniosacral therapy massage is typically performed with the client fully clothed and lying down on a massage table. The therapist may use a light touch or hold different areas of the body to help facilitate the release of tension and stress.

Lymphatic Drainage Massage

Lymphatic drainage massage is a type of massage that is designed to help promote lymphatic flow and drainage. The lymphatic system is responsible for helping to remove toxins and waste from the body, but it can become sluggish or blocked, which can lead to swelling and other health problems.

During a lymphatic drainage massage, the therapist uses gentle, rhythmic strokes and pressure to stimulate lymphatic flow and help remove excess fluid from the tissues. This can be helpful in treating conditions such as lymphedema, post-surgical swelling, and other types of edema.

Lymphatic drainage massage can also help to boost the immune system and improve overall health and well-being. It is typically a gentle and relaxing form of massage that can be performed on its own or in conjunction with other types of massage therapy.

Myofascial Release Massage

Myofascial release massage is a type of massage therapy that focuses on releasing tension and tightness in the fascia, a connective tissue surrounding muscles and organs in the body. Myofascial release massage aims to improve the range of motion, reduce pain, and enhance overall well-being by working on the fascia and soft tissue restrictions. During the massage, the therapist applies gentle, sustained pressure to areas of tension in the fascia, using a variety of techniques such as stretching, compression, and deep tissue massage. This type of massage can be beneficial for those who experience chronic pain, limited mobility, or postural imbalances. It can also be used as a preventative measure to maintain optimal health and function of the body.

Neuromuscular Therapy Massage

A neuromuscular therapy massage is a specialized form of

177

massage therapy that focuses on the treatment of muscular and nervous system problems. It involves using pressure and friction to manipulate soft tissue to relieve pain and dysfunction caused by nerve compression, muscle imbalances, or other issues.

This type of massage therapy is often used to treat conditions such as chronic pain, sports injuries, and muscle spasms. The therapist will work to identify areas of muscular tension and trigger points and use various techniques to release the tension and restore normal muscle function.

Neuromuscular therapy massage can be a highly effective form of treatment for those with chronic pain or muscular dysfunction. It can help to improve circulation, reduce inflammation, and promote healing in injured or damaged tissues. Additionally, many people find that this type of massage can help alleviate stress and promote relaxation, improving overall physical and mental well-being.

Rolfing Massage

Rolfing massage, also known as Structural Integration, is a type of massage therapy that focuses on improving the body's alignment and balance. It is based on the idea that the body's structure and function are interrelated and that improving its alignment can help improve its overall function and reduce pain and discomfort.

Rolfing massage typically involves a series of sessions, each focusing on a different area of the body. The therapist will use a variety of techniques, such as deep tissue massage and stretching, to help release tension and realign the body's structure.

Rolfing massage can be helpful in treating a variety of conditions, including chronic pain, back pain, and posture problems. It can also be used to improve athletic performance and enhance overall well-being.

Geriatric Massage

Geriatric massage is a type of massage specifically designed for elderly clients. It is a gentle and slow massage that takes into account the unique physical and emotional needs of older adults. Geriatric massage can help improve circulation, reduce pain and stiffness, and promote relaxation. It may also help alleviate symptoms of conditions common in older adults, such as arthritis, hypertension, and dementia. The massage therapist may use light stretching, gentle kneading, and joint mobilization techniques to help improve flexibility and mobility. Communication with the client is especially important during geriatric massage to ensure their comfort and safety.

Hydrotherapy Massage

Hydrotherapy massage is a type of massage that involves the use of water, either in the form of hot or cold water, to enhance the massage experience. Hydrotherapy can be used in conjunction with other massage techniques to help reduce pain, swelling, and muscle tension. One popular form of hydrotherapy massage is called a "hydrotherapy massage bed," a water-filled cushion that allows the client to float and be massaged simultaneously. Other hydrotherapy massage forms may involve using water jets or a hot tub to help relax and soothe sore muscles. Hydrotherapy can be particularly beneficial for those with arthritis, fibromyalgia, or other chronic pain conditions, as well as athletes recovering from injuries or overexertion.

Understanding the various types of massage therapy and their benefits is essential for any massage therapist. By deeply understanding the different techniques, massage therapists can tailor their services to meet each client's specific needs, providing a more effective and satisfying massage experience.

Providing Customized Services That Meet the Needs Of Your Clients

Providing customized services is an essential part of running a successful massage therapy business. Every client is unique, with different needs and preferences, so it's important to tailor your services to meet those needs. By providing personalized services, you can help your clients feel valued and cared for and increase their likelihood of returning to your business in the future.

Customized services are important for several reasons. Firstly, they allow you to provide more effective massage treatment. By understanding your client's specific needs, you can target areas of tension and pain more effectively and provide a massage that is more likely to provide relief. Additionally, providing customized services can help build trust and rapport with your clients, as they feel you are taking the time to understand their unique needs.

There are several ways to provide customized services that meet the needs of your clients. First, it is important to take the time to understand your client's medical history and any current health conditions they may have. This can help you tailor your massage techniques to avoid aggravating any existing injuries or conditions. Additionally, you can ask your clients about their preferences for pressure, temperature, and any areas they would like to focus on during their massage.

Another way to provide customized services is to offer a variety of massage techniques so that clients can choose the one that best meets their needs. For example, if a client is experiencing chronic pain, you might recommend a deep tissue massage, whereas a Swedish massage might be more appropriate if they are looking for relaxation.

Finally, it's important to listen to your client's feedback and make adjustments to your services as needed. Encourage your clients to provide feedback after each session, and use that feedback to improve your services in the future. By providing customized services that meet the needs of your clients, you can build a loyal customer base and establish yourself as a trusted and effective massage therapist.

Create a Comfortable and Relaxing Environment That Enhances the Massage Experience

Creating a comfortable and relaxing environment is essential to enhancing the massage experience for your clients. It involves considering the sensory experience, such as lighting, sound, and temperature, as well as the physical comfort of your clients. A comfortable environment helps put clients at ease and allows them to fully relax, enhancing the therapeutic benefits of the massage. It can also help to create a sense of trust and safety, which is important in building strong client relationships.

Personalization is a key aspect of creating a comfortable and relaxing environment for your clients. By getting to know your clients and their individual preferences, you can tailor the massage experience to meet their specific needs. This can include things like music or scent preferences, the amount of pressure they prefer, or specific areas of the body they want you to focus on. By personalizing the massage experience, you are not only showing your clients that you value their individual needs, but you are also able to provide a more effective and enjoyable massage. When clients feel that their preferences and needs are being taken into account, they are more likely to relax and fully engage with the massage, leading to better results and increased satisfaction.

To personalize the massage experience, start by asking your clients about their preferences and any specific areas of concern they may have. Take note of their responses and adjust your approach accordingly. You may also want to offer various options, such as different types of music or scents, so clients can choose what works best for them. By consistently providing a personalized and tailored massage experience, you can build strong relationships with your clients and earn their loyalty and repeat business.

Ensuring a clean and hygienic environment is crucial to creating a comfortable and relaxing massage experience for your clients. A clean environment helps prevent the spread of germs and bacteria and promotes a sense of calm and tranquility. To ensure that your massage space is clean and hygienic, it's important to regularly sanitize all surfaces, including massage tables, chairs, and any equipment that is used during the session. This includes using disinfectant sprays or wipes on surfaces, washing linens between clients, and using fresh towels or blankets for each session.

It's also important to have proper ventilation in the massage room to promote air circulation and prevent stuffiness. This can be achieved by opening windows, using fans, or installing an air purifier. In addition to cleaning and ventilation, it's important to maintain a clutter-free environment. A cluttered space can be distracting and may cause anxiety for clients, which can detract from the massage experience. Keeping the space organized and free from clutter can help create a sense of calm and promote relaxation.

Maintaining a comfortable temperature in the massage room is essential to creating a relaxing environment. The temperature should be set at a level that is comfortable for the client, and if necessary, additional heating or cooling options should be provided. For example, a heated blanket or warmer might be available during colder months to keep the client warm. Conversely, a fan or air conditioning system can help keep the room cool and comfortable during the hot summer months.

It's also important to ensure that the temperature is consistent throughout the massage. Sudden temperature changes can disrupt the relaxation and comfort of the client. By maintaining a consistent temperature, you can help ensure that the client is able to fully relax and enjoy the massage experience.

Continuing to seek feedback from clients and making improvements to the environment is a crucial aspects of creating a comfortable and relaxing atmosphere. As a massage therapist, it is important to regularly check in with your clients to see if there are any areas that could be improved or if they have any specific needs or preferences. This can be done through a simple conversation or through the use of feedback forms. Based on this feedback, you can make appropriate changes to the environment to enhance the client's experience. For example, if clients consistently mention that the lighting is too bright, you can adjust the lighting to a softer, more calming level. Similarly, if clients express discomfort due to the temperature, you can adjust the temperature control accordingly. By continually seeking feedback and making improvements to the environment, you demonstrate a commitment to providing the best possible massage experience for your clients. This not only helps build a loyal client base but can also lead to positive word-of-mouth referrals and a strong reputation in the industry.

By creating a comfortable and relaxing environment, you can help your clients fully immerse themselves in the massage experience and enhance the therapeutic benefits of the massage. This can lead to satisfied clients who are more likely to return and recommend your services to others.

Continuing Your Education and Professional Development To Stay Up-To-Date With The Latest Techniques And Trends In Massage Therapy

Continuing education and professional development are essential for any massage therapist who wants to stay up-to-date with the latest techniques and trends in massage therapy. It not only helps you provide better services to your clients but also enhances your career prospects. As a massage therapist, you should aim to broaden your knowledge and skills in various areas, such as anatomy, physiology, kinesiology, and pathology, to name a few. This will help you better understand the body's functions and how massage therapy can address different health concerns.

Continuing education can also help you keep up with the latest advancements in massage therapy, such as new techniques, tools, and technologies. It will help you remain competitive and stand out in the industry. Moreover, attending conferences, workshops, and seminars can help you network with other professionals and gain exposure to different ideas and perspectives.

To stay up-to-date with the latest trends in massage therapy, you can also explore new areas of practice, such as sports massage, prenatal massage, or geriatric massage. These areas of specialization can help you cater to specific client needs and preferences. Overall, continuing education and professional development are crucial for massage therapists who want to grow and excel in their careers. It allows you to offer the best services to your clients, improve your skills and knowledge, and stay current with the latest developments in the industry.

Chapter Eleven

Balancing Work and Life

Welcome to Chapter 11 of The Ultimate Guide to Building a Successful Massage Therapy Business. In this chapter, we will explore the importance of balancing work and life to maintain health and well-being and avoid burnout. As a massage therapist, managing a busy practice and maintaining a fulfilling personal life can be challenging. However, it is essential to prioritize self-care and create a sustainable work-life balance to achieve success in both areas.

This chapter will discuss key strategies for balancing work and life, including effective time management, prioritizing self-care, and creating a sustainable schedule that allows you to achieve your business goals without sacrificing your personal life. By implementing these strategies, you can create a healthy, sustainable balance between your work and personal life while avoiding burnout and maintaining your own health and well-being. Whether you are a seasoned massage therapist or just starting out, the strategies outlined in this chapter will be invaluable for achieving long-term success and fulfillment in both your professional and personal life. So, let's dive in and discover how to balance work and life as a massage therapist.

Balancing work and life is crucial to achieving success in

both your professional and personal life. The demands of running a massage therapy business can often lead to long working hours and high levels of stress, which can negatively impact your physical and mental health. In order to maintain your own health and well-being and avoid burnout, it is important to prioritize and manage your time effectively. In the following sections, we are going to explore several key strategies for balancing work and life.

Managing Your Time Effectively by Creating a Schedule and Sticking To It

Managing your time effectively is crucial for maintaining a healthy work-life balance. One of the best ways to manage your time is by creating a schedule and sticking to it. This involves setting aside specific blocks of time for work, exercise, self-care, and other activities that are important to you.

By creating a schedule, you can ensure that you dedicate enough time to each area of your life and not neglect anything. It can also help you avoid overcommitting yourself and feeling overwhelmed. Sticking to your schedule is equally important, as it helps you develop good habits and ensures that you are making progress toward your goals. Here are some elements of a good schedule:

- Clearly defined tasks and priorities

- Time for self-care: A good schedule should also include time for self-care activities, such as exercise, meditation, or spending time with loved ones. Taking care of oneself is essential for maintaining health and avoiding burnout, and it should be a priority in any schedule.

- Communication with colleagues and clients to ensure availability and manage expectations

- Flexibility: While it's important to have a schedule and stick to it as much as possible, it's also important to have some flexibility built in for unexpected situations or emergencies that may arise.

- Realistic time estimates: It's important to be realistic about how long certain tasks or appointments will take to avoid overbooking or running behind schedule.

- Prioritization: The most important tasks or appointments should be scheduled during the time of day when you are most productive and focused.

- Buffer time: It can be helpful to schedule buffer time between appointments or tasks to allow for breaks, travel time, or unexpected delays.

- Regular review and adjustment: Schedules should be regularly reviewed and adjusted as needed to ensure they remain effective and manageable.

However, unexpected events or emergencies can arise, and it's important to be able to adapt to changing circumstances without sacrificing your overall work-life balance. With practice, effective time management can become a habit and make a significant difference in your overall health and well-being.

Taking Breaks and Prioritizing Self-Care to Avoid Burnout and Maintain Your Own Health and Wellbeing

Taking regular breaks and prioritizing self-care is essential for maintaining your physical and mental health as a massage therapist. The demanding nature of the job can lead to burnout and fatigue if proper self-care practices are not implemented. Taking breaks throughout the day is important to rest, recharge, and refocus. This can include short breaks between clients, as well as longer breaks for meals or physical activity. Use these breaks to engage in activities that help you relax and reduce stress, such as stretching, deep breathing, or mindfulness practices.

In addition to taking breaks, prioritize self-care practices that promote overall health and well-being. This can include regular exercise, proper nutrition, and sufficient sleep. Make time for activities that bring you joy and relaxation, such as hobbies or spending time with loved ones. Remember that self-care is not selfish or indulgent but rather a necessary aspect of maintaining your health and wellbeing. By prioritizing self-care and taking breaks, you can avoid burnout and continue providing your clients the best possible care. The following are some self-care ideas that can help you avoid burnout and maintain your well-being:

1. Taking regular breaks to rest and recharge
2. Practicing mindfulness and meditation to reduce stress and anxiety
3. Engaging in physical activity or exercise to promote physical and mental health
4. Eating a balanced and nutritious diet to fuel your body and mind
5. Getting enough sleep allows your body to rest and rejuvenate
6. Engaging in activities that bring you joy and fulfillment, such as hobbies or spending time with loved ones
7. Seeking support from a therapist or counselor to manage stress and maintain mental health
8. Saying no to commitments or responsibilities that may cause excessive stress or overwhelm
9. Engaging in self-reflection and setting boundaries to prioritize your own needs and well-being.

Incorporating self-care practices into your daily routine can be challenging, especially when your schedule is busy. However, by setting aside time each day to prioritize your health and well-being, you can create sustainable habits that will benefit both you and your clients in the long run.

Creating a Sustainable Work-Life Balance That Allows You to Achieve Your Business Goals Without Sacrificing Your Personal Life

Creating a sustainable work-life balance is a crucial component of achieving success in both your personal and professional life. It means prioritizing self-care and taking the necessary steps to manage your time and energy effectively. Without a healthy balance between work and life, you risk experiencing burnout, decreased productivity, and decreased quality of life. It can also negatively impact your relationships with loved ones and your overall well-being.

To create a sustainable work-life balance, start by identifying your priorities and values in both your personal and professional life. Set realistic goals for both areas and create a schedule that allows you to allocate time and energy to each. Practice effective time management strategies, such as delegating tasks and avoiding multitasking. Prioritize self-care activities, such as exercise, meditation, or spending time with loved ones. Learn to say no to commitments that don't align with your priorities or cause excessive stress. Seek support from friends, family, or a therapist if necessary. Remember that creating a sustainable work-life balance is a continuous process and requires regular adjustments to meet your changing needs and priorities.

In conclusion, balancing work and life is a vital component of maintaining your own health and well-being and avoiding burnout as a massage therapist. It can be challenging to manage a busy practice while also maintaining a fulfilling personal life, but it's essential to prioritize self-care and create a sustainable work-life balance to achieve success in both areas. In this chapter, we explored key strategies for balancing work and life, including effective time management, prioritizing self-care, and creating a schedule that allows you to achieve your business goals without sacrificing your personal life. By implementing these strategies, you can create a healthy, sustainable balance between your work and personal life while avoiding burnout and maintaining your own health and well-being.

Remember, creating a schedule that works for you and incorporating self-care practices into your daily routine takes time and effort. It requires setting realistic goals, communicating effectively with colleagues and clients, and regularly reviewing and adjusting your schedule as needed. Taking regular breaks, prioritizing self-care, and creating a sustainable work-life balance is essential for achieving long-term success and fulfillment in both your professional and personal life.

Balancing work and life is a continuous process, but with practice and dedication, you can achieve a healthy and sustainable balance that will benefit both you and your clients. By prioritizing your own well-being, you can provide the best possible care to your clients and build a successful and fulfilling massage therapy business. Thank you for joining us in this chapter, and we hope that the strategies outlined here will help you achieve a healthy and sustainable work-life balance.

Chapter Twelve

Managing Your Business Risks

Welcome to Chapter 12 of The Ultimate Guide to Building a Successful Massage Therapy Business. This chapter will explore the importance of managing your business risks to protect your business and ensure its long-term sustainability. As a massage therapist, your business is your livelihood, and it's important to identify and manage potential risks to minimize the impact of unexpected events. You can protect your business and safeguard your financial future by implementing key strategies for managing your business risks.

This chapter will discuss several key strategies for managing your business risks, including identifying potential risks, developing contingency plans, and obtaining appropriate insurance coverage. We will also explore common types of business risks and their potential impact on your massage therapy practice. Understanding and managing these risks can protect your business and position yourself for long-term success.

The first step in managing your business risks is to identify potential risks to your business. This can include natural disasters, equipment failures, and data breaches, among others. Once you have identified potential risks, you can develop contingency plans to respond to emergencies and unexpected events. This may involve developing a plan for responding to a power outage, natural disaster, or other unexpected event that could disrupt your business operations.

In addition to developing contingency plans, obtaining appropriate insurance coverage for your business is important. This can include liability insurance to protect against potential lawsuits, as well as business interruption insurance to provide financial support in the event of an unexpected interruption to your business operations.

By implementing these key strategies for managing your business risks, you can protect your business and ensure its long-term sustainability. Understanding and managing your business risks is essential for success in the massage therapy industry. So, let's dive in and discover how to effectively manage your business risks as a massage therapist.

Identify Potential Risks to Your Business

Identifying potential risks to your massage therapy business is an essential step in managing your business risks. One potential risk that can have a significant impact on your business is natural disasters. Natural disasters, such as hurricanes, earthquakes, floods, and wildfires, can cause damage to your business property, disrupt operations, and lead to financial losses. You can develop a plan to mitigate the impact by identifying potential risks, such as natural disasters, and preparing for the unexpected. Failing to prepare for natural disasters can devastate your business, so it's essential to assess the potential risks and develop a plan to address them.

In addition to natural disasters, there are a variety of other risks that can pose a threat to your massage therapy business. These risks can vary depending on the nature of your business and your industry. It's important to identify potential risks and develop strategies for managing them in order to protect your business and ensure its long-term sustainability.

One common risk that massage therapists may face is the risk of injury or liability claims from clients. While massage therapy is generally a low-risk practice, accidents can happen, and clients may file claims against your business. It's important to have appropriate liability insurance coverage in place to protect your business from financial losses in the event of a claim.

Another potential risk to your business is the loss of key employees or contractors. If a key employee or contractor were to leave your business suddenly, it could impact your ability to provide quality services to clients and could also lead to a loss of revenue. It's important to have contingency plans in place for employee departures, such as having a plan for training and hiring new staff.

Cybersecurity is also becoming an increasingly important concern for businesses of all sizes, including massage therapy businesses. With the rise of digital technology, businesses are becoming more vulnerable to data breaches, hacking, and other forms of cyberattacks. It's important to take steps to protect your business from these risks, such as implementing strong passwords and data encryption, backing up important data regularly, and regularly updating your computer systems and software.

Other potential risks to your business may include changes in industry regulations, economic downturns, or unexpected events such as pandemics or political upheavals. By identifying potential risks and developing strategies for managing them, you can protect your business and ensure its long-term sustainability.

Here are some steps to identify potential risks to your business:

1. **Conduct a comprehensive risk assessment:** This involves evaluating all areas of your business and identifying potential risks. Areas to consider include your physical premises, equipment, staff, clients, suppliers, and other stakeholders.

2. **Gather relevant information:** Collect as much information as possible about potential risks to your business, such as local weather patterns, crime rates, and market trends.

3. **Brainstorm potential risks:** Gather input from

employees, stakeholders, and industry experts to identify potential risks that may not have been immediately apparent.

4. **Evaluate the likelihood and potential impact of each risk:** Assess the likelihood of each risk occurring and the potential impact it could have on your business. This will help you prioritize which risks to focus on.

5. **Create a risk register:** Document all identified risks, including their likelihood and potential impact, in a risk register. This will help you track and manage risks over time.

6. **Continuously review and update the risk register:** Regularly review and update the risk register as new risks emerge or existing risks change in likelihood or impact.

Here are some steps to identify potential risks to your business related to natural disasters:

7. **Research natural disaster risks in your area:** Research the potential natural disaster risks in your area, such as hurricanes, earthquakes, floods, or wildfires. Understanding the specific risks in your area can help you develop a more targeted plan to address them.

8. **Review your insurance coverage:** Review your

insurance coverage to ensure that you are adequately protected in case of a natural disaster. Consider obtaining additional insurance coverage, such as flood insurance, if necessary.

9. **Develop a contingency plan:** Develop a contingency plan that outlines the steps you will take in the event of a natural disaster. This should include emergency procedures, such as evacuation plans, communication plans with clients and employees, and a plan to resume operations after the disaster.

10. **Maintain and update your plan:** Your contingency plan should be regularly reviewed and updated to ensure it remains effective and relevant. Make sure all employees are aware of the plan and trained to follow the emergency procedures.

By taking the time to identify potential risks to your business, you can develop strategies to mitigate or manage them effectively, protecting your business and ensuring its long-term sustainability.

Developing Contingency Plans for Emergencies and Unexpected Events

Developing contingency plans for emergencies and unexpected events is an important part of managing business risks. Contingency planning involves preparing for potential disruptions to your business operations and developing a plan of action to mitigate their impact. By creating a contingency plan, you can minimize the impact of unexpected events and maintain business continuity.

A contingency plan outlines the actions you will take in the event of an unexpected event or emergency. It should include a list of potential risks and scenarios and the steps to take to address each situation. Contingency plans should be tailored to your specific business needs and potential risks. Developing a contingency plan helps you to be prepared for unexpected events that can disrupt your business operations. Whether it's a power outage, natural disaster, or another unforeseen event, having a plan in place can help you minimize the event's impact and continue to operate your business.

The following steps can help you to develop a contingency plan for your business:

1.   **Identify potential risks:** Identify potential risks to your business, such as natural disasters, power outages, or other unexpected events. Consider the likelihood and impact of each potential risk.

2.   **Assess the impact:** Let's say that a potential risk to your massage therapy business is a power outage. If a power outage were to occur, it could impact your ability to provide services to clients, store and access client

information, and process payments. Assessing the potential impact of this risk on your business operations will help you to prioritize your contingency planning efforts and focus on the most significant risks.

3. **Develop a plan of action:** To address the risk of a power outage, you may develop a plan of action that outlines steps to minimize the impact on your business operations. This may include investing in a backup generator, ensuring all client information is stored securely and accessed offline, and having alternative payment methods available.

4. **Communicate the plan:** Once you have developed a contingency plan for a potential risk like a power outage, it is important to communicate it to all relevant employees, stakeholders, and partners. This ensures that everyone is aware of their roles and responsibilities in the event of an emergency and can work together effectively to minimize the impact on your business operations.

5. **Test the plan:** To ensure that your contingency plan is effective and up-to-date, it is important to test it regularly. For example, you could simulate a power outage and run through your plan to identify any potential issues and make necessary adjustments. By

testing your plan regularly, you can ensure that you are prepared for any unexpected events that may arise and minimize the impact on your business operations.

Developing a contingency plan is an important step in managing your business risks. By being prepared for unexpected events, you can minimize the impact on your business operations and ensure continuity of service for your customers.

Obtaining Appropriate Insurance Coverage for Your Business

Obtaining appropriate insurance coverage for your business is essential for protecting your business against potential risks and liabilities. Insurance coverage can provide financial protection in the event of unexpected events or accidents, such as property damage, lawsuits, or natural disasters. Your business may be vulnerable to financial loss and potential closure without the right insurance coverage. Let's discuss the importance of obtaining appropriate insurance coverage for your business and how to go about getting it.

Obtaining appropriate insurance coverage for your business is crucial for protecting your assets and ensuring your long-term sustainability. Various types of insurance coverage are available for businesses, depending on the nature of your business and the potential risks you may face. Some common types of insurance coverage include general liability insurance, property insurance,

203

workers' compensation insurance, and professional liability insurance.

General liability insurance covers a broad range of potential risks, such as bodily injury, property damage, and advertising injury. Property insurance provides coverage for damage or loss to your business property, including buildings, equipment, and inventory. Workers' compensation insurance provides coverage for employees who are injured or become ill on the job. Professional liability insurance, also known as errors and omissions insurance, provides coverage for businesses that offer professional services, such as legal or financial advice.

Obtaining appropriate insurance coverage can provide numerous benefits for your business, including financial protection, peace of mind, and legal compliance. Insurance coverage can provide financial protection against unexpected events and accidents that could otherwise result in significant financial loss or liability. It can also provide peace of mind by reducing the potential for financial hardship and allowing you to focus on your business operations. Additionally, obtaining appropriate insurance coverage can help your business comply with legal requirements and contractual obligations.

You can obtain appropriate insurance coverage for your business by completing several steps, including identifying the types of insurance coverage you need, researching insurance providers, and comparing coverage options and pricing. It's important to work with a reputable insurance provider that specializes in insurance coverage for your specific industry or business type. Be sure to review policy terms and conditions carefully, including coverage limits, deductibles, and exclusions. Reviewing your insurance coverage regularly and making any necessary adjustments as your business grows or changes is also a good idea.

In conclusion, managing your business risks is essential for the long-term sustainability of your massage therapy practice. Chapter 12 of The Ultimate Guide to Building a Successful Massage Therapy Business discussed several key strategies for managing business risks, including identifying potential risks, developing contingency plans, and obtaining appropriate insurance coverage. By implementing these strategies, you can protect your business and position yourself for success.

Identifying potential risks to your business is an essential step in managing your risks as an entrepreneur. From natural disasters to data breaches, there are a variety of risks that can pose a threat to your massage therapy business. By identifying potential risks, you can develop strategies to mitigate or manage them effectively.

Developing contingency plans for emergencies and

unexpected events is also crucial for managing business risks. By creating a contingency plan, you can minimize the impact of unexpected events and maintain business continuity. Testing your plan regularly can ensure that you are prepared for any unexpected events that may arise.

Obtaining appropriate insurance coverage for your business is essential for protecting your assets and ensuring your long-term sustainability. Insurance coverage can provide financial protection against unexpected events and accidents that could otherwise result in significant financial loss or liability. It can also help your business comply with legal requirements and contractual obligations.

In summary, managing your business risks is an ongoing process that requires careful planning, preparation, and execution. By implementing the strategies discussed in Chapter 12, you can protect your business and position yourself for long-term success in the massage therapy industry.

Chapter Thirteen

Building Your Network

Building a strong network is essential for growing your massage therapy business. You need to connect with other massage therapists and healthcare professionals, build relationships with potential referral sources, and utilize networking events to grow your business. Key strategies for building your network include:

- Joining local and national massage therapy associations to connect with other professionals in your industry
- Building relationships with healthcare professionals, such as chiropractors and physical therapists, who can refer clients to your business
- Utilizing networking events and social media to connect with potential clients and grow your business

Chapter Fourteen

Navigating Legal and Regulatory Requirements

In Chapter 14, we will dive into an important part of the massage business: Navigating Legal and Regulatory Requirements for Massage Therapy Businesses. Understanding the legal and regulatory landscape of the massage therapy industry is crucial for protecting your business and avoiding legal issues that could harm your reputation and financial stability. This chapter will provide you with key strategies for navigating legal and regulatory requirements, including the importance of consulting with a lawyer to ensure you understand the legal requirements for your business, obtaining necessary licenses and permits such as a massage therapy license or business license, and complying with relevant laws and regulations such as HIPAA and OSHA regulations.

By implementing these strategies, you can protect your business, minimize legal risks, and ensure compliance with all relevant regulations. This chapter will provide you with the tools and knowledge you need to navigate the legal and regulatory landscape of the massage therapy industry. Join us as we explore the crucial topic of navigating legal and regulatory requirements for massage therapy businesses and learn how to protect your business, comply with relevant laws and regulations, and ensure your long-term success.

Navigating the legal and regulatory requirements for massage therapy businesses is essential for protecting your business and avoiding legal issues. You need to understand the legal and regulatory requirements for your industry, obtain necessary licenses and permits, and comply with relevant laws and regulations. Let's explore several key strategies for navigating legal and regulatory requirements include.

Consult with A Lawyer To Ensure You Understand The Legal Requirements For Your Business

Consulting with a lawyer is essential in ensuring you understand the legal requirements for your massage therapy business. A lawyer can provide you with valuable advice and guidance on the laws and regulations that apply to your business and help you navigate the complex legal landscape. So, why is it important to consult with a lawyer when starting or running a massage therapy business? The answer is simple: legal compliance. Failure to comply with relevant laws and regulations can lead to fines, lawsuits, and even the closure of your business. As a massage therapist, it's essential to understand the legal requirements for your business and take steps to ensure compliance.

But navigating the legal landscape can be challenging, especially if you don't have a legal background. That's where a lawyer can help. A lawyer can provide you with the expertise and knowledge you need to understand the legal requirements for your business and help you develop a plan to ensure compliance.

So, how do you go about consulting with a lawyer? The first step is to find a lawyer who specializes in business law or has experience working with massage therapy businesses. Here are some resources for finding an attorney:

1. **Referrals from other business owners:** Ask other business owners in your industry for recommendations on attorneys they have worked with.

2. **Bar associations:** Local or state bar associations can provide referrals to attorneys specializing in your business area.

3. **Online legal directories:** Websites such as Avvo or Martindale-Hubbell provide directories of attorneys based on their location and practice areas.

4. **Legal aid societies:** Nonprofit legal aid societies can provide referrals to low-cost or pro bono attorneys for small business owners who cannot afford traditional legal fees.

5. **Business organizations:** Many business organizations, such as chambers of commerce or industry associations, offer legal referral services for their members

6.   **Local law schools:** Law schools often have legal clinics where law students provide legal services under the supervision of licensed attorneys.

It's important to do your research and choose an attorney who has experience working with businesses in your industry and who you feel comfortable working with. Once you've identified a lawyer, schedule a consultation to discuss your business and the legal requirements that apply to it. During the consultation, the lawyer will ask questions about your business and provide information on the legal requirements you need to comply with.

Obtaining Necessary Licenses and Permits

Obtaining the necessary licenses and permits is an essential step in setting up a massage therapy business. This includes obtaining a massage therapy license and a business license. Obtaining the necessary licenses and permits is important for several reasons. First, it ensures that you operate legally and in compliance with state and local laws and regulations. Second, it can help you build credibility with clients, as they will know that you have met the necessary requirements and standards to operate a professional massage therapy business. Finally, it can help protect you from potential legal and financial issues that may arise from operating without the necessary licenses and permits.

Obtaining the necessary licenses and permits can be a

straightforward process, but it can vary depending on the state and local regulations in your area. The following are some general steps that you can take to obtain the necessary licenses and permits:

1. Researching the requirements for licenses and permits is a critical step in starting a massage therapy business. It is important to know the specific requirements for your area and industry so that you can ensure that your business is in compliance with all relevant regulations. Failure to comply with licensing and permit requirements can result in penalties, fines, and even the closure of your business.

To start the research process, you should consult with local and state licensing agencies to determine the specific requirements for massage therapy businesses in your area. You can also check online resources or speak with other massage therapists in your community to gain insight into the process.

The requirements for a massage therapy license can vary by state but typically include completing a certain number of training hours, passing an exam, and submitting an application with relevant fees. In addition to a massage therapy license, you may also need to obtain a business license and any other relevant permits, such as a permit for operating a home-based business or for providing services in a certain area.

Researching the requirements for licenses and permits can

be time-consuming, but it is a crucial step in starting your massage therapy business on the right foot. Make sure to take the time to understand the requirements for your area and ensure that you are in compliance with all relevant regulations.

2. Completing the necessary education or training is important in obtaining a massage therapy license. In many states, massage therapists are required to complete a certain amount of education or training before they can be licensed. This is to ensure that they have the necessary knowledge and skills to provide safe and effective massage therapy services to their clients.

The specific requirements for education and training vary depending on the state or jurisdiction. Some states require a minimum number of classroom hours, while others may allow for online or distance learning. Additionally, some states may require massage therapists to pass a certification exam before being licensed.

It is important to research the specific requirements in your area and ensure that you are completing the necessary education or training. This may involve enrolling in a massage therapy program at an accredited institution, completing online courses or workshops, or attending continuing education courses to maintain your license.

By completing the necessary education or training, you can

213

ensure that you have the knowledge and skills to provide high-quality massage therapy services to your clients while also meeting the legal requirements for obtaining a massage therapy license.

3. Submitting an application for a massage therapy license and/or a business license is the final step in obtaining the necessary permits to legally operate your massage therapy business. It's important to carefully review the application requirements and ensure you have all the necessary documentation and information before submitting your application.

Some of the information that may be required on the application includes your personal and business information, proof of education and training, proof of insurance, and any other relevant documents or certifications. Depending on your area, fees may also be associated with submitting your application.

It's important to note that the application process may take some time, so it's important to plan accordingly and submit your application as early as possible. Once your application has been submitted, it will be reviewed by the appropriate regulatory agency, and if approved, you will receive your massage therapy license and/or business license. With these permits in hand, you can legally operate your massage therapy business and provide your clients with the highest quality of care.

4. Obtaining a massage therapy license and/or a business license may involve paying certain fees. These fees vary by state and region, so it is important to research the specific fees required in your area. These fees can include application fees, licensing fees, and renewal fees. Budgeting accordingly for these fees is essential to ensure that your business can operate legally and without interruption. Some states may also require additional fees for background checks, fingerprinting, or continuing education courses. Be sure to research all the necessary fees in advance so that you can plan and budget accordingly for them.

5. After submitting your application and paying the required fees, the next step is to wait for approval from the regulatory agency. It is important to keep in mind that the processing time for approval can vary depending on the location and the agency handling the application. Typically, the approval process may take several weeks or even months. During this time, it is important to be patient and follow up with the regulatory agency if necessary. Once you receive approval, you will be able to legally operate your massage therapy business in compliance with the necessary licenses and permits.

By following these steps and obtaining the necessary licenses and permits, you can ensure that you operate legally and comply with state and local laws and regulations. This can help you build client credibility and protect your business from legal and financial issues.

Complying With Relevant Laws and Regulations, Such as HIPAA And OSHA Regulations

Complying with relevant laws and regulations is crucial for the success of your massage therapy business. Two essential regulations you need to comply with are HIPAA and OSHA. HIPAA stands for Health Insurance Portability and Accountability Act. A federal law in the United States establishes privacy and security standards for protecting personal health information.

OSHA stands for Occupational Safety and Health Administration. It is a federal agency in the United States that sets and enforces safety and health standards for the workplace to ensure the safety and well-being of workers. Compliance with HIPAA and OSHA regulations ensures that your client's information is kept confidential and that your workplace is safe and healthy for both clients and employees. Failing to comply with these regulations can result in legal issues, fines, and reputational damage.

To comply with HIPAA regulations, you need to:

- Develop and implement a privacy policy that outlines how you handle clients' protected health information (PHI).

- Train your staff on HIPAA regulations and the importance of protecting clients' PHI.

- Obtain signed consent forms from clients before disclosing their PHI to third parties.

- Securely store and dispose of clients' PHI to prevent unauthorized access.

To comply with OSHA regulations, you need to:

- Identify and assess potential hazards in your workplace and take steps to mitigate them.

- Train your staff on how to use equipment safely and how to respond to emergencies.

- Maintain accurate records of workplace injuries and illnesses.

- Provide your staff with personal protective equipment (PPE) and ensure they use it appropriately.

Overall, complying with relevant laws and regulations, such as HIPAA and OSHA regulations, is essential for the success and sustainability of your massage therapy business. By understanding the requirements and taking the necessary steps to comply, you can protect your clients, your employees, and your business.

In conclusion, navigating legal and regulatory requirements is an essential step in establishing and maintaining a successful massage therapy business. This chapter has provided key strategies for understanding legal requirements, obtaining necessary licenses and permits, and complying with relevant laws and regulations such as HIPAA and OSHA regulations. By following these strategies, you can protect your business, minimize legal risks, and ensure compliance with all relevant regulations.

Consulting with a lawyer is crucial for understanding the legal requirements for your business and developing a plan to ensure compliance. Obtaining necessary licenses and permits, including a massage therapy license and business license, is essential for operating legally and building credibility with clients. Compliance with relevant laws and regulations such as HIPAA and OSHA is crucial for protecting your clients and employees and avoiding legal issues.

By implementing the strategies outlined in this chapter, you can confidently navigate the legal and regulatory landscape of the massage therapy industry and ensure your business's long-term success.

Chapter Fifteen

Scaling Your Business for Growth

Welcome to Chapter 15 of The Ultimate Guide to Building a Successful Massage Therapy Business, where we will explore the exciting topic of scaling your business for growth. If you're a massage therapy business owner, you know how important it is to continually grow and expand your business to stay competitive and achieve long-term success. But with so many different strategies and approaches to growth, it can be challenging to know where to start.

This chapter will provide you with key strategies and insights into scaling your massage therapy business for growth. We'll explore how to identify opportunities for growth and expansion, develop a growth strategy that aligns with your business goals and values, and create a plan for long-term sustainability and success. By following these strategies, you can take your massage therapy business to the next level and achieve your desired growth and success.

One of the essential aspects of scaling your business for growth is identifying expansion opportunities. This could involve offering new services, targeting new markets, or even expanding into new geographic areas. By identifying opportunities for growth, you can tap into new revenue streams and expand your customer base, ultimately increasing your profitability and success.

However, identifying opportunities for growth is just the first step. To achieve sustainable growth and success, you must develop a growth strategy aligning with your business goals and values. This involves considering your business's unique strengths, weaknesses, opportunities, and threats and developing a plan that leverages these factors to achieve your growth objectives.

Finally, creating a plan for long-term sustainability and success is crucial for achieving sustainable growth and success. This involves managing your finances, managing your employees effectively, and investing in your business to ensure continued growth and profitability. By following these key strategies, you can scale your massage therapy business for growth and achieve long-term success and sustainability. Join us as we explore these strategies and provide you with the tools and knowledge you need to take your massage therapy business to the next level.

Identifying Opportunities for Growth and Expansion

Identifying opportunities for growth and expansion is essential for scaling your business and achieving long-term success. As a massage therapist, you may be looking for ways to grow your business and reach new clients. One effective strategy is to offer new services or target new markets.

So, why is it important to identify opportunities for growth and expansion? The answer is simple: stagnation. If you don't continue to innovate and grow, your business may become stagnant, and you may miss out on potential opportunities for growth and success. Offering new services is one way to attract new clients and expand your business. For example, if you currently offer only massage therapy services, you may consider adding services such as acupuncture, yoga, or other wellness services. By diversifying your services, you can attract a wider range of clients and increase your revenue streams.

Another strategy for identifying opportunities for growth and expansion is to target new markets. For example, if you currently only serve individual clients, you may consider expanding to corporate wellness programs or offering services to athletes or other specialized groups. By targeting new markets, you can reach new clients and expand your business in exciting new ways.

But how do you go about identifying new opportunities for growth and expansion? The first step is to analyze your current business and identify areas where you can improve or expand. You may also want to research industry trends and emerging markets to identify potential opportunities. Once you've identified potential areas for growth and expansion, you can develop a plan to implement new services or target new markets. This may involve investing in new equipment, hiring additional staff, or marketing your business in new ways.

Overall, identifying opportunities for growth and expansion is crucial for scaling your massage therapy business and achieving long-term success. By offering new services or targeting new markets, you can attract new clients and expand your business in exciting new ways.

Developing A Growth Strategy That Aligns with Your Business Goals And Values

Developing a growth strategy that aligns with your business goals and values is essential for achieving long-term success and sustainability. It's not enough to simply identify opportunities for growth and expansion; you need to have a clear plan for achieving your growth objectives in a way consistent with your overall vision and mission.

So, what exactly does it mean to develop a growth strategy that aligns with your business goals and values? At its core, it means taking a thoughtful and intentional approach to growth, one that considers not only the potential financial benefits of expanding your business but also the impact that growth will have on your employees, customers, and community.

Why is it so important to align your growth strategy with your business goals and values? The answer is simple: growth for growth's sake is not always a recipe for success. If you pursue growth opportunities without considering how they fit into your

222

broader business strategy and values, you may end up overextending yourself or making decisions that are not in the best interests of your business or your stakeholders.

On the other hand, a growth strategy aligned with your goals and values can help you stay focused on what matters most to your business and ensure that your growth objectives align with your overall vision and mission.

So, how do you develop a growth strategy that aligns with your business goals and values? The first step is to clearly define your business goals and values. What is your overall vision for your business, and what core values guide your decision-making? Once you have a clear understanding of your goals and values, you can begin to identify growth opportunities that are consistent with them.

For example, if one of your core values is sustainability, you may want to focus on growth opportunities that are environmentally friendly or that promote social responsibility. Or, if your goal is to become a leader in your industry, you may want to focus on developing new products or services that set you apart from your competitors.

The next step is to develop a growth plan that outlines how you will achieve your growth objectives in a way consistent with your goals and values. This may involve investing in new technology or equipment, expanding your team, or partnering with other businesses or organizations. Whatever growth strategies you choose, it's important to keep your goals and values in mind and ensure that your decisions are in line with them.

Finally, monitoring your progress and adjusting your growth strategy as needed is important. This may involve revisiting your goals and values periodically to ensure they are still relevant and guiding your decision-making or making changes to your growth plan based on customer or stakeholder feedback.

By developing a growth strategy that aligns with your business goals and values, you can ensure that your business is not just growing for growth's sake but that it's growing in a way consistent with what matters most to you and your stakeholders. With a clear plan in place, you can move forward with confidence, knowing that you are on the path to long-term success and sustainability.

Creating A Plan for Long-Term Sustainability And Success By Managing Your Finances, Managing Your Employees, And Investing In Your Business

Creating a long-term sustainability and success plan is crucial for any business owner. To achieve long-term success, you need to have a solid plan that takes into account various factors such as financial management, employee management, and investing in your business. Creating a plan for long-term sustainability and success involves several key components, including managing your finances, managing your employees, and investing in your business. These components work together to ensure your business remains successful and profitable for years.

Managing your finances is a crucial aspect of running a successful business. It involves monitoring and analyzing your financial performance to make informed decisions about your company's future. Without a solid understanding of your financials, it can be challenging to make the right decisions that can lead to long-term success.

You need to start by tracking your revenue, expenses, profits, and cash flow to effectively manage your finances. This information can be used to create a budget and forecast future financials. You can use financial statements such as balance sheets, income, and cash flow statements to clearly understand your company's financial health. Once you understand your financials well, you can use this information to make informed decisions about investments, pricing, and other critical aspects of your business. For example, if you notice that your expenses are higher than your revenue, you may need to look for ways to cut costs or increase sales. On the other hand, if you see that your profits are increasing, you may consider investing in new equipment or hiring additional staff to grow your business.

Managing your employees is critical to the long-term success of your business. Your employees are not just resources but valuable assets that can contribute to your business's growth and success. As a business owner, you must create an environment that fosters productivity, creativity, and innovation. This can be achieved by developing a positive workplace culture that aligns with your business goals and values.

Creating a positive workplace culture means creating an environment that promotes open communication, collaboration, and mutual respect. This can be achieved by treating your employees with dignity and appreciation and recognizing their hard work and contributions. Additionally, providing ongoing training and development opportunities can help employees develop new skills, stay engaged, and grow within the company.

Setting clear expectations and goals is also essential to effective employee management. By establishing clear goals, employees can focus on what needs to be done and what success looks like. Additionally, setting expectations helps to ensure that everyone is on the same page and working towards the same objectives. When employees understand what is expected of them, they are more likely to stay motivated, focused, and productive.

Effective employee management is crucial to the success of

any business, and it involves more than just setting clear expectations and providing ongoing training. Offering competitive benefits and compensation packages, such as health insurance, retirement plans, and performance bonuses, can help attract and retain top talent in your industry. Additionally, providing a safe and comfortable working environment can improve employee morale and productivity, leading to better business outcomes. By giving employees opportunities for career advancement within your company, you can also foster a sense of loyalty and commitment among your workforce, which can contribute to long-term success. Effective employee management ultimately involves creating a positive workplace culture that values and supports your employees, which can translate into increased customer satisfaction and profitability for your business.

Investing in your business is essential for long-term success and growth. Whether it's upgrading your technology, expanding your product line, or renovating your facilities, investing in your business can help you stay ahead of the competition and meet the changing needs of your customers. When you invest in your business, you show your commitment to its future success. By regularly assessing the needs of your business and making smart investments, you can position your company for continued growth and profitability. This can include hiring new employees, investing in research and development, or purchasing new equipment. By investing in your business, you can also create new opportunities for revenue growth. For example, expanding your product line allows you to tap into new markets and reach new customers. Alternatively, by upgrading your technology or facilities, you can improve the efficiency of your operations and reduce costs, which can translate into higher profits.

Ultimately, investing in your business is an investment in your future. By making strategic investments and staying ahead of the competition, you can position your company for long-term success and growth.

Assessing your current financial situation is an essential first step in creating a plan for long-term sustainability and success. By carefully reviewing your revenue and expenses, you can better understand your financial position and identify areas where you can improve. First, start by gathering your financial records, including your income statements, balance sheets, and cash flow statements. Use this information to create a detailed financial analysis of your business. Look for trends and patterns in your revenue and expenses, and identify any areas where you may be overspending or underperforming.

Once you clearly understand your financial situation, it's time to create a budget that aligns with your business goals. This budget should include all of your anticipated revenue and expenses for the upcoming year, as well as any contingencies or unexpected expenses that may arise. When creating your budget, be sure to consider both short-term and long-term goals for your business. This may include investing in new equipment, hiring additional staff, or expanding your services or product offerings. By aligning your budget with your business goals, you can ensure that you are investing in the right areas and setting yourself up for long-term success.

Investing in ongoing training and development opportunities is also crucial for employee management. Providing your employees with the tools and resources they need to improve their skills can help them grow in their roles and contribute to the success of your business. By creating a clear path for career advancement within your business, you can also encourage your employees to stay with your company for the long term. Effective employee management can help you create a positive workplace culture, retain talented employees, and achieve long-term success. Listen to your employees' feedback and ideas, and continue investing in their growth and development.

Finally, investing in your business is essential for achieving long-term success and sustainability. As you assess your financial situation and manage your employees effectively, it's crucial to identify opportunities for growth and expansion. This could involve launching new products or services that meet the needs of your target market, targeting new markets to reach a wider audience, or upgrading your facilities and equipment to improve efficiency and productivity. By investing in your business, you can stay ahead of the competition, create new revenue streams, and continue to grow and expand. However, developing a growth strategy that aligns with your business goals and values is important. This involves conducting research, analyzing market trends, and understanding the needs and preferences of your target audience.

Once you've identified opportunities for growth and expansion, create a plan for long-term sustainability and success. This should include managing your finances effectively, managing your employees, and investing in your business. By taking a strategic approach and focusing on these key areas, you can achieve long-term success and build a thriving, sustainable business. By taking these steps, you can create a plan for long-term sustainability and success that will help your business thrive for years to come.

Conclusion:

In conclusion, building a successful massage therapy business takes more than just technical skills in massage therapy. It requires a comprehensive understanding of business practices and strategies. You can attract clients and build a strong online presence by defining your business goals, creating a solid business plan, developing a strong brand, and implementing effective marketing and promotion strategies. Pricing your services appropriately, managing your finances, and hiring and managing employees are also essential components of a successful massage therapy business. You can create a sustainable business by providing high-quality services, managing client relationships, balancing work and life, and navigating legal and regulatory requirements. Finally, by identifying opportunities for growth and expansion, developing a growth strategy that aligns with your business goals, and creating a plan for long-term sustainability and success, you can scale your business for growth and achieve long-term success. By following the strategies outlined in this book, you can create a business that provides exceptional services, builds strong relationships with clients, and achieves long-term success and sustainability.

About the Author

Maurice C. Hill is a man of many talents and experiences, including that of a former Adjunct Professor at Mercer University College of Professional Advancement and a decorated sailor who served in the United States Navy during the first Gulf War. Maurice's dedication to his country and service in the Navy instilled in him the values of discipline, teamwork, and commitment, which he continues to uphold in his personal and professional life.

After completing his military service, Maurice began his academic journey by earning undergraduate degrees in Business Administration and Education from Georgia State University. He later earned a Bachelor's degree in Business Management and a Master's degree in Business Administration from the University of Phoenix. Maurice's passion for counseling individuals and families led him to pursue a Master's degree in Clinical Mental Health Counseling from Mercer University, where he also studied Counselor Education and Supervision while in a Ph.D. program.

Maurice's vast knowledge and experience in various fields have made him a sought-after authority in his respective areas. He is currently a licensed real estate broker and a licensed professional counselor (LPC) in the state of Georgia, a National Certified Counselor (NCC), a member of the Dekalb Board of Realtors, the Georgia Association of Realtors, and the National Association of

Realtors. Maurice began his real estate career in 1997 and later became the chief executive officer (CEO) and qualifying broker of All Properties Professionals Realty in East Point, Georgia. He also serves as the founder and CEO of One United Publishing, where he helps business owners achieve their goals and aspirations through self-help books.

Maurice's dedication to helping others extends beyond his professional life. While in graduate school with a focus on training master's level clinical mental health counselors, Maurice became concerned about helping budding entrepreneurs who desire to own and operate their businesses. Inspired by the strong desire and sense of urgency related to helping business owners, Maurice decided to apply for and eventually enroll in the Harvard University entrepreneurship program. With his combined education and experience as an educator, business owner, and counselor, Maurice decided to write a group of self-help books.

Maurice has lectured nationally and internationally on various topics related to mental health counseling, including Vicarious Trauma, the Psychological Aspects of Multiculturalism in Counseling, and Trauma-Focused Cognitive Behavioral Therapy. He has been honored with numerous awards throughout his career, including The Empire Board of Realtist Million Dollar Club Award from 2000-2006 and the Dekalb Board of Realtors Pinnacle Award in 2020, 2021, and 2022. He is also a member of the Chi Sigma Iota International Honor Society.

In addition to his professional accomplishments, Maurice is an avid traveler who has visited nearly 30 countries. His experiences abroad have enriched his understanding of humanity and the natural world. Studying the diverse cultures, histories, and socio-political landscapes of the places he has visited have deepened his love for humanity and nature. These experiences have opened his eyes to the complexity and beauty of our world and have inspired him to be a lifelong learner and advocate for positive change.

Maurice C. Hill is a remarkable individual who has impacted the lives of many through his passion, dedication, and expertise. His unwavering commitment to helping people achieve their goals and aspirations inspires others. With extensive knowledge and experience in multiple fields, Maurice is highly regarded as an authority and sought-after speaker. Additionally, Maurice has pursued his passion for flying airplanes by training at the Aviation Career Enrichment Inc in Atlanta, Georgia. His love for adventure and exploration, coupled with his dedication to his work, make him an inspiration to all. When he's not up in the air, Maurice enjoys spending quality time with his family.

Made in the USA
Middletown, DE
26 November 2023

43594149R00141